成语故事百咏

（英汉对照）

100 Chinese Idioms and Their Stories

编著　杨增强

译　张翔真

审校　朱莉安·威廉斯

(Julianne Williams)

插图　沈友斌

金盾出版社

内 容 提 要

本书采用英汉对照的形式把100个成语典故改写成100首叙事诗，读起来合辙押韵，朗朗上口，是学习普及成语典故知识、提高英语学习兴趣和阅读能力的新尝试。所选的成语，故事性强，使用频率高，多见于中小学语文教材和报刊，好懂易记。本书适用于中学生以及具有初等以上英语水平的读者。

图书在版编目(CIP)数据

成语故事百咏(英汉对照)/杨增强编著；张翔真译. — 北京：金盾出版社，2013.7

ISBN 978-7-5082-8337-1

Ⅰ.①成… Ⅱ.①杨…②张… Ⅲ.①英语—汉语—对照读物②汉语—成语—故事 Ⅳ.①H319.4：I

中国版本图书馆CIP数据核字(2013)第083639号

金盾出版社出版、总发行

北京太平路5号(地铁万寿路站往南)

邮政编码：100036 电话：68214039 83219215

传真：68276683 网址：www.jdcbs.cn

封面印刷：北京印刷一厂

正文印刷：双峰印刷装订有限公司

装订：双峰印刷装订有限公司

各地新华书店经销

开本：787×1092 1/32 印张：10.25 字数：296千字

2013年7月第1版第1次印刷

印数：1～5 000册 定价：23.00元

序

生活在中国是一种神奇的文化体验，而分享在这个古老国度里亲眼目睹、亲身体验其灿烂文化和生活方式的机会却相对较少。因此，通过将中书英译让更多的人了解和认识中国文化和生活是一种非常有益的尝试。

有幸的是我能有机会审校这本先用汉语写成然后翻译成英语的精彩故事书。

讲述传统故事，无论是民间故事或神话，是任何一个国家文化的重要组成部分，这本精彩的《成语故事百咏（英汉对照）》就充分地证明了这一点。通过这些故事，大家可以更好地了解这些汉语成语的出处。英译本可使那些愿意花些时间读读这本书的人更好地理解中国文化的丰厚底蕴。

对于我们这些不会汉语的人来说，这样的书是非常有价值的。每个故事的历史时期和文化背景赋予每个成语深刻的历史含义，中国历史的悠久和丰富由此可见一斑。

我希望这本书的读者，能同我们几位编写、翻译和审校的人一样得到同样的快乐和兴致。

朱莉安·威廉斯

Foreword

Living in China is an amazing cultural experience. The opportunity to see firsthand the life styles and to share in the amazing tapestry that is China, such an ancient nation, is shared by comparatively few. To increase this awareness with so many other people through the production of Chinese books translated into English, is a worthwhile endeavour.

One of the greatest opportunities offered to me has been the chance to examine and proof this wonderful book that was written firstly in Chinese and then translated into English.

The retelling of traditional stories, be they folk tales or myths, is an important part of any country's culture. This is especially true of this charming book, "100 Chinese Idioms and Their Stories". Through these stories it is possible to gain a greater understanding and awareness of where so many Chinese idioms are founded. The translation of such a book into English allows the richness of Chinese culture to have greater meaning for those who take the time to enjoy it.

For those of us unable to read the Chinese language, such a book is invaluable. Each story places its characters in a time period and cultural setting giving an historical meaning to their content. China's history is both ancient and rich as we can see in its story telling.

I hope this book bring as much enjoyment and interest to those who read it, as was gained by those of us who worked on it.

by Julianne Williams, English Tutor from Australia, 2000—2004, Wuxi, China

地缘文化与全球文化的融合(代序)

人类的思想和文化通过语言文字传承着,从时代上来说,老子、孔子、孟子等圣贤先哲与我们相隔两千多年了,我们通过读他们的书在继承着中华民族的文化;而从地缘上来说,中国文化的发源地距离我和杨增强先生的家乡新沂——苏鲁豫皖四省交界处非常接近,我们的方言里至今还保留着许多古代文化信息。所以当读《诗经·硕鼠》时就得到了意外的惊喜,原来它的韵脚就是我们苏北地区方言的发音:"硕鼠硕鼠,无食我麦(měi)!三岁贯汝,莫我肯德(děi)。逝将去汝,适彼乐国(guǐ)。乐国乐国,爰得我直。"由此我猜想,孔子当年讲话大概是带着鲁南和苏北口音的。

在当今全球化、信息化时代,文化和信息跨越时空,逐渐被整合到一个五光十色的国际化平台。基于这个理念,我们几个人尝试着把这些折射着中国古代智慧光芒的成语以讲故事的形式传播出来。

在苏北和鲁南等很多地区我们所喜闻乐见的一个曲艺形式就是山东快书,虽说它具有浓重的地方色彩,但它却有着深厚的历史背景。本书的中文部分就是由杨增强先生借助这种具有地缘特色的传统韵诵体诗歌编写而成，叙事手法简洁明快，语言生动活泼，故事讲得有声有色。相信一定会给中外读者留下深刻印象，读来也定会受益匪浅。

英文部分由我仿照美国诗人惠特曼的“用音步不用韵脚”的风格，将我多年收听收看《空中英语教室》学到的成语、习语和惯用法等融合在故事叙述中，虽然没有像原文那样押韵脚，但却尽量照顾了内韵和节奏，使故事读起来颇有点英语古体诗的味道。英语译文完成后，承蒙澳大利亚英语专家朱莉安·威廉斯女士（2000—2004年任职于中国无锡某教育机构）的悉心审校，文字更加精准和洗练，相信本书英文可作为广大大中学生、英语爱好者很好的阶进读物。

当然，英语译文中也难免会存在一些疏漏，欢迎读者和专家提出宝贵意见，以便我们把弘扬中华文化这项工作做得更好。

张翔真

CONTENTS 目录

目　录

目　录

一、按图索骥

古时候有个伯乐会相马，
写了部相马的经书传天下。
书中讲，好马脖高眼睛亮，
四腿高长蹄子大。
哪知他，生个儿子太愚笨，
读死书，不求甚解糊涂瓜。
有一天，这孩子田里去玩耍，
捉了只特大的蛤蟆捧回家，
“爸爸、爸爸”连声叫，
“快来看，这有一匹最好的马！
像你讲的脑袋像你说的腿，
眼睛明亮圆又大！
别看它皮外无毛疙瘩多，
它可是又能蹦来又会爬！”
伯乐一见心好恼，
可也拿儿子没办法。
“孩子啊，你看问题太简单，
难怪今天闹笑话。
你捉的若是好马就骑试试，
我怕你难以驾驭它！”
这孩子眨巴着双眼开了窍，
一撒手放了那只癞蛤蟆，

让它回田里捉害虫，
消灭害虫保庄稼。
到后来，“按图索骥”作成语，
常比喻，做事拘泥旧成法；
也比喻，寻找事物有线索，
避免盲目乱抓瞎。

Look for a Steed with the Aid of Its Picture

Once there was an old man by the name of Bo Le, who was quite good at judging horses. He wrote a book on it and it was of great value. If the neck is high and the eyes are bright, it is a very good steed, the book says. If the legs are long and the hooves are big, it is a very good steed, the book says. But the man had a son who was not quite as clever. Though he loved to read, he could hardly grasp anything. One day, while the boy was playing in the fields, he caught hold of a very big toad and went running home.

"Dad, dad," he called out, "come and take a look, I've got the best steed in the world. The head is tall and the legs are long, the eyes are bright and round and large, just like you wrote in the book. Although he has no hair and has a spotted hide, he can jump and crawl along as well."

Bo Le become annoyed at what he saw, but there was nothing he could do with his stupid son.

"My dear child, you are very single-minded, no wonder today you made a serious mistake. If it were a good horse, why didn't you get on its back. I fear you could not manage it." At this the child seemed to understand and let go of the big toad. "Let it go to the corn field to kill the pests who might eat the crops otherwise."

Hence it came into being this idiomatic phrase. It means "to do just as it is shown to be", or "in doing something you must try to use common sense, avoiding a blind and careless mistake."

二、杯弓蛇影

晋朝时有个乐(yuè)广很好客，
有一次把一位知心朋友请到家，
摆上了美酒和佳肴，
饮酒叙说知心话。
忽然间客人见杯中乱蠕动，
分明是一条小蛇在杯里趴，
小蛇儿曲曲弯弯真吓人，
便怀疑是朋友存心想害他。
那乐广殷勤敬酒没在意，
朋友却推说酒醉要回家。
各样的珍馐(xiū)美味不愿尝，
临别时闷闷不乐没说话。
回家后郁郁寡欢生了病，
那乐广知道以后倍惊讶，
他专到朋友家里去探望，
朋友却不愿把实情告诉他。
回家后乐广坐客位仔细瞧，
见一把常用的角弓墙上挂。
又把那酒杯斟满放原处，
弓影儿落在酒杯无偏差。
他这才知道朋友得病因，
赶快去又把朋友请到家。

恳切地让他坐在原位上，
接着把弓影落杯细细拉。
那朋友恍然大悟疑惧消，
方晓得杯中蛇影原是假。
到后来"杯弓蛇影"作成语，
比喻人疑神疑鬼生惧怕。

A Snake Shadow in a Cup

There was a hospitable man whose name was Yue Guang in the Dynasty of Jin(265—420A. D.). One day, he invited one of his friends to dinner in his home. Having put on the table various expensive wines and delicious dishes, they sat drinking and talking delightfully. All of a sudden the guest caught sight of something wriggling in his cup. Apparently it was a little snake, twisting and turning, a fearful snake in his wine cup.

It must be evil. The guest thought that Yue Guang meant to do harm to him. Yue Guang was busy toasting him and didn't notice what was going on. The guest pretended to be drunk and said he had to be going. He did not taste a variety of dishes on the table and he made very few remarks when he said good-bye.

The guest got seriously ill after he returned home. Yue Guang was very surprised when he heard this, and he paid a hearty visit to his piteous friend.

The friend however, would not tell him the truth. Yue Guang went home and sat in the same seat his friend took that eventful day. He noticed the bow he often used, hanging on the wall. He filled the cup with wine and put it in the very same place. He saw the shadow of the bow in the wine cup exactly like a live snake. Now he knew the real cause of his friend's illness. He immediately invited the friend to his home again, and asked him to sit in that very seat, and he made him see the shadow of the bow in the wine. At last his friend came to know what was wrong. The horrible snake was simply the shadow of the bow!

The idiom "A Snake Shadow in a Cup" came to mean that someone was apt to feel doubtful and very timid.

三、闭门思过

今日山东郓城地，
西汉时候称东郡。
当时有个韩延寿，
曾在东郡做太守。
部下劝告能听取，
经常采纳好建议。
东郡治理非常好，
延寿因此有名气。
一直在那做太守，
后来调到左冯翊(yì)，
即今陕西大荔州，
头几年，从未到各县去巡视。
有一次一个部下提醒他，
劝他下去走一走，
了解民情怎么样，
以及各县啥政绩。
延寿说，各县官长很贤明，
下属也能勤效力，
巡视恐怕没必要。
那位部下不服气，
连说正当春耕时，
可以看看耕种事。

延寿一想也在理，
随即收拾出城去。
到了高陵县境内，
告状来了俩兄弟，
只因互相争田产，
请求延寿给评理。
对此事，延寿心中生感触，
他认为，百姓争端责在己。
自己身为父母官，
教化百姓有不及。
有伤风情与教化，
贤人孝子以为耻。
想到此，他决定让贤要退职，
称病不再理政事。
地方官员见此情，
深感自身也失职。
就连那互争田地的兄弟俩，
也来认罪各责己。
延寿以酒来款待，
对他们知过悔过多勉励。
延寿复出又重理政，
二十四县都巡及。
下属及百姓更敬重，
从此再无争讼事。
到后来“闭门思过”作成语，

常与闭门自省的行为比。
自知之明是美德，
人人难免犯过失，
能够自我作批评，
对自身修养最有益。

Pondering Behind a Closed Door

In the present Yuncheng County, Shandong Province which was called Dongjun during the Western Han Dynasty (206B. C. —24A. D.), there was a person named Han Yanshou, who was viceroy of the district. He always kept himself advised, and often adopted his subordinates' constructive suggestions. In this way Dongjun was run very well.

By and by, Yanshou was well-known for his advisability, and so he continued to be a good viceroy. Later he was transferred to Zuofengyi, the present Dalizhou of Shaanxi① Province. There he made no inspections in the first few years. One day a subordinate of his reminded him about going around and making an inspection to learn how the people lived, and what the county leaders had accomplished.

---

① 1979 年以来，"山西"和"陕西"被约定俗成地拼写成："Shanxi"和"Shaanxi"，以示区别。

"Officers of each county are able and wise," Yanshou said, "and their staff are also diligent, so the inspection would be of little value."

His subordinates did not agree with him, and said that since it was spring plowing time he could at least go and see how the peasants sow. This, Yanshou thought might make some sense, so he got prepared and set out immediately.

He came to Gaoling County, where two brothers sued each other and entered the court, quarreling about their inherited land. They begged Yanshou to decide who was right and who was wrong. Yanshou was feeling quite upset about this, as he regarded it as his own fault. As an official in charge of this place, he hadn't done well enough in educating and moralizing upon his people. A gentleman could not live down the shame of it, when he found out something was indecent and immoral.

Upon thinking this, he decided to resign from his post. And so he pretended to be ill and shunned his duties. When the officials of the district saw this they took it as their own fault. And even the two quarreling brothers confessed their misdoings respectively.

Then Yanshou entertained them with good wine in praise of their acknowledgment and repentance. After that Yanshou resumed his post, and made a thorough inspection throughout the 24 counties. Now

his subordinates and his people spoke highly of him. There were no more quarrels or suing from that time.

Later, the idiom "Pondering Behind a Closed Door" came to mean that "one should look before he leaps" or "be careful and always behave well". Self-knowing is a moral thing, because everyone is apt to make mistakes. If you constantly try self-criticism, you'll be next to the saints someday.

四、别开生面

唐朝时皇宫设有“凌烟阁”，
此阁着实不简单。
唐太宗开国功臣二十多，
画像都挂在“凌烟阁”里面。
转眼过了上百年，
到玄宗时，肖像的颜色已暗淡，
有的面目已模糊，
辨认是谁很困难。
有个画家叫曹霸，
绘画的技巧很精湛，
擅长画战马和人像，
幅幅活灵又活现。
有人说他是曹操的后代，
玄宗封他将军衔。
为了重画功臣像，
玄宗勉励曹霸重任担，
经过曹霸努力后，
功臣像原貌又重现，
甚至比原画还要好，
体现在配色描摹多方面。
大诗人杜甫见后很佩服，
专门赋诗把曹霸赞：

"凌烟功臣少颜色，
将军笔下开生面"。
到后来，"别开生面"作成语，
常形容创造了新的形势与局面。

Better Than the Original

In the Royal Palace of Tang Dynasty (618—907A. D.) there was a building named "Over-Smoke Pavilion", which was very famous at that time. In the reign of Taizong, there had hung more than 20 portraits of the founders of the Dynasty. Months ran into years and years into decades. When it came to Xuanzong's reign, the color of the portraits had already faded. Some had even lost the complexions in their faces, and it was very hard to tell who was who.

There was an artist by the name of Cao Ba, who was very accomplished at his skills. He was so good at drawing warring horses and people, that he could make them vivid and lifelike.

Xuanzong was told that Cao Ba was the descendant of Cao Cao, so he made him a general. Having wanted to refresh the portraits of the heroes, Xuanzong encouraged Cao Ba to take up the task. After much painstaking effort, the portraits were new and lifelike again, and to some extent

they were better than before, in their coloring and line-drawing etc.

The then great poet Du Fu, admired him when seeing the painting, and wrote a poem to praise him: "The heroes in the Over-Smoke Pavilion were losing their colors, but beneath the general's brush they became better than the original." The phrase "better than the original" became an idiom, denoting a new situation is created or a new phase has been turned.

五、不觉技痒

战国时，燕国艺人高渐离，
会演奏叫做“筑”的古乐器。
他击筑技艺非寻常，
因此大大有名气。
高渐离荆轲偶相遇，
二人一见如故成知己，
常聚在燕都酒店开怀饮，
击筑唱歌抒胸臆。
过不久，燕太子请荆轲助他刺秦王，
史书清楚将这故事记。
据说那荆轲离开燕国上路时，
送行的，便是太子和高渐离。
送别送到易水河，
渐离动情把筑击。
乐声凄怆令人悲，
“易水悲歌”传后世。
哪料想，荆轲行刺事未成，
先在秦国被杀死。
秦王动怒发大兵，
攻伐燕国捉太子。
荆轲同党受牵连，
高渐离，改名换姓远逃离。

到一个荒僻山乡做佣工，
主人丝毫也不知。
有一次，主人设宴请宾客，
酒席间，有人助兴把筑击。
高渐离听了筑乐耐不住，
对那人击筑技巧作评议。
真不愧行家里手有见地，
在座的，没有一个不服气。
主人又请他即席作表演，
直奏得喝彩之声时时起。
谁料到，这一演奏了不得，
竟有人，认出他就是高渐离！
渐离丝毫不惧怕，
开箱子，拿出了
自己珍藏的好乐器。
同时换上旧时装，
不顾一切献筑技。
主人宾客惊又喜，
从此不以佣工视，
待以客礼照顾周，
无人出卖去告密。
渐离击筑成佳话
“不觉技痒”作成语，
常比喻，身怀高超技艺者，
逢机会，总会跃跃作尝试。

Itching to Have a Go

During the period of the Warring States (475—221B. C.), there was a man named Gao Jianli in the State of Yan, who was quite good at playing the ancient musical instrument *zhu*. And because of his amazing skill, he was then very well-known.

One day, he made friends with a man named Jing Ke, and they became sworn friends forever. They drank in the city's restaurant, and played *zhu* to express their hearts. Before long, the prince of the State of Yan asked Jing Ke to assassinate the Emperor of Qin. (You probably know the story in Chinese history.) It was said that the men who sent Jing Ke off were none other than the prince and Gao Jianli. They saw Jing Ke off at the Yishui River, where Jianli played *zhu* emotionally. So emotional and so sad was the music, that "Sad Songs by the Side of the Yishui River" was passed down for generations.

Unfortunately, Jing Ke failed to assassinate the Emperor of Qin and was killed in Qin. The Emperor of Qin got so furious that he attacked the State of Yan and tried to capture the prince. Jing Ke's followers were in grave trouble. Gao changed his name, and ran to a faraway village to work as a tenant peasant, whose landlord knew nothing about it.

One day, the landlord prepared a feast for his

guests. During the feast, the instrument *zhu* was played to entertain the guests. On hearing the beautiful music of the *zhu*, he couldn't help making comments on the striker's skill. His critical comments were so professional that everyone present was impressed. The host then asked him to give a performance, which won him great applause. But alas, his real identity was then laid bare. While he conscientiously played the zhu, Gao Jianli was not afraid at all. Whereupon he opened his trunk, and took out his dear instrument that was hidden until now. He dressed in his old-fashioned costume, and fearlessly started to play.

The host and guests were surprised and overjoyed, and no longer treated him as a servant, but as an honorable guest instead. No one wanted to turn traitor against him, only to keep a delightful secret.

"Itching to have a go" as an idiom, is usually used to refer to those who have good skills and are always longing to give a show.

六、不食周粟

西汉时，
司马迁著了部史书叫《史记》，
有一篇《伯夷列传》很有趣。
讲的是殷商时有个孤竹国，
那国君，年老临终把遗嘱立，
他想让小儿子叔齐继大位。
叔齐他年纪虽小却懂道理，
他说是长兄伯夷该继位，
这本是祖宗立下的老规矩。
伯夷说父命不可违，
反复再三让叔齐。
兄弟二人互推让，
谁也不愿把位即。
兄弟俩，先后逃出王宫去，
只好由另一个兄弟把王位继。
时光倏忽几十载，
伯夷叔齐又巧遇。
原来是西伯姬昌已去世，
儿子姬发把位继，
姬发便是周武王，
弟兄俩决定投他去。
周武王看到商朝已衰落，

起兵征讨不迟疑。
弟兄二人得知后，
拦住马头齐劝阻。
武王不听紧催兵，
攻下商都周朝立。
哪知晓，伯夷叔齐不高兴，
认为那殷纣再坏是天子。
周武王不过是个诸侯王，
臣子灭君是篡逆。
更何况武王还有不孝罪，
兴兵之时父刚逝。
对待武王新政权，
伯夷叔齐不服气，
死抱着君、臣、父、子旧伦理，
对新生事物瞧不起。
弟兄俩双双躲进首阳山，
每日里，只是野果野菜来充饥。
大周朝，粟米虽多偏不食，
兄弟俩，竟然活活被饿死。
临终前，唱着一首自编的歌，
《采薇》便是诗歌题，
大意是："登上西山采野菜，
君王残暴不可取。
可惜啊，周武讨伐商纣王，
以暴易暴惹人急。

暴臣以暴待暴君，
尧舜之世已远去。
我们何处去安身？
不遇明君宁饿死。
不食周粟是我志，
饿死自认命不济。”
到后来，“以暴易暴”作成语，
常形容，残暴势力互代替。
伯夷叔齐恨姬发，
此恨绝对无道理。
不明事理太固执，
饿死实在不足惜。
“不食周粟”作成语，
竟转为，形容做人有骨气。

Refuse to Eat Zhou's Food

In the Western Han Dynasty (206B. C.—24A. D.), Sima Qian wrote an historical book entitled "Records of the Historian", in which there was a very interesting story about Bo Yi.

It says that in the State of Guzhu in Yin-Shang Dynasty (1766—1122B. C.), the old king made a will before he died, and he would let his youngest son Shu Qi inherit the throne. Shu Qi, young as he was, was quite ritualistic. He said that his eldest brother, Bo Yi

should have the throne, as it was the old rule passed down from their forefathers.

The two brothers bandied the offer with each other, and neither would take the legacy. The two brothers ran away from the palace, only to leave one of the other brothers to take the throne.

Time flew and decades went by. Bo Yi and Shu Qi met again. It happened that Xibo Jichang, the king had just died, and his son Jifa had inherited the throne. Jifa was none other than King Wu of Zhou Dynasty.

The two brothers wanted to go to him. King Wu of Zhou Dynasty noticed that the Shang Dynasty was on the decline, so he launched an attack on it without hesitation. When the two brothers heard the news, they grabbed his horse by the head and tried to stop him. But King Wu paid no heed to them and ordered his soldiers to hurry. Soon he overthrew the Shang Dynasty and set up a new Dynasty, Zhou.

The two brothers Bo Yi and Shu Qi were disappointed, and thought that though Yinzhou was a bad king after all he was the son of Heaven. Wu was but a Duke, and it was a usurpation for a subject to dethrone a ruler. And what was more Duke Wu committed the crime of disloyalty. No sooner had his father died than he summoned his army.

The two brothers disdained Wu's new authority.

Holding onto the old theory of king-and-minister-father-and-son, they looked down upon all the new things. Both the brothers hid in the Shouyang Mountain. They picked wild plants to eat for their daily food, while the Zhou Dynasty abounded in food, and they starved themselves to death.

Before dying, they sang a song composed by themselves, "Picking Wild Plants" was the title. It ran like this: "Having climbed the western hills to pick wild plants, A violent tyrant was no good; It is a worry that a tyrant replaced another tyrant, Times of Yao and Shun were gone forever, And where can we find a place to live? We'd rather starve to death as we haven't met a wise king. Refusing to eat Zhou's food, that is our will. And starving to death, we regard it our fate." Later "Replace a Tyrant with a Tyrant" as an idiom, expresses the meaning that cruel power comes to the place of another cruel power. While Bo Yi and Shu Qi were considered stubborn and inflexible, "Refusing to Eat Zhou's Food" as an idiom, means that one has quite a backbone.

七、草菅人命

西汉时文帝幼子叫刘胜，
小时候生得很聪明。
文帝因此最爱他，
打算皇位让他承。
当时有贾谊文学大名家，
曾遭诽谤排挤离京城，
在长沙王那儿任太傅。
用人才，文帝又把他召进京。
这时候刘胜已封梁怀王，
汉文帝特让贾谊教刘胜。
贾谊想不仅要教他会读书，
还要让他把做人道理学通明。
秦末的赵高也教过秦二世，
只教他酷法和严刑，
学的是如何砍头割鼻子，
和怎样夷灭三族索人命。
到后来胡亥即位就乱杀戮，
把人命看得像草叶一样轻。
贾谊说，
二世杀人如割草，
并非是胡亥天生恶本性，
赵老师未能领他走正道，

秦末才有楚汉争。
贯太傅一心要教好梁怀王，
哪料想天有不测灾祸生，
刘胜骑马不小心，
马上摔下丧了命。
贾谊自觉失了老师职，
经常流泪心悲痛。
过了几年忧郁死，
后人提起总伤情。
到后来贾谊说的那句话，
演化为成语“草菅人命”，
意思是把人命当作菅草待，
常把统治者杀戮无辜的罪恶来形容。

To Kill People Like Cutting Clover

In the Western Han Dynasty (206B. C. —24A. D.), Emperor Wen had a little son named Liu Sheng, who was very clever when he was a child. Emperor Wen liked him very much, and decided to let him inherit his throne.

At that time, there was a famous scholar, Jia Yi, who had been slandered and expelled from the capital city. Jia was later a secretary to the Lord of Changsha. Wendi decreed his return to the palace to tutor

his favorite son Liu Sheng, who had been appointed Lord of Lianghuai.

Jia Yi thought that he should not only teach him how to read and write, but also teach him how to conduct himself. Another scholar Zhao Gao at the end of the Qin Dynasty (221—206B. C.) tutored Qin II, but only taught him to make hard laws and to persecute the people. He taught him how to behead and cut off noses, and how to slaughter three generations of a household.

Qin II Hu Hai then began to kill people when he came to power, and he regarded human lives as grass leaves. Jia said the reason why Qin II killed people like cutting grass, was not because he was born to be evil, but because his teacher had taught him so. This led to the conflict between the States of Chu and Han.

With this in mind, Master Jia whole-heartedly wanted Lord Lianghuai to be a good emperor. But what man proposes, God disposes. Liu Sheng one day made a blunder while riding, and unfortunately fell dead from the horseback.

Jia Yi felt guilty as a teacher, and he often shed tears sadly. A few years later he died a melancholy death. The people were sad when they later mentioned it.

The utterance made by Jia Yi, had changed into "to Kill People Like Cutting Clover", which means to

regard people's lives as grass, as to depict a tyrannical government who savagely kills innocent people.

八、诚惶诚恐

东汉成皋有任县令叫杜诗，
这人大大有来历：
他少年即胸怀大志气不凡，
很快就官升侍御史。
有一位将军萧广很蛮横，
经常放纵士兵把百姓欺。
敲诈勒索钱与物，
有时还蹿进村中抢妇女。
老百姓受到骚扰生怨愤，
杜诗就找到萧广把这事提，
劝诫他以后不能再这样，
萧广却根本不当一回事。
杜诗一怒之下动了手，
杀死了萧广方解气。
把萧广的罪行公布后，
老百姓欢天又喜地。
光武帝刘秀得知后，
颁下圣旨召杜诗，
对他的果敢倍赞赏，
给杜诗升官赠棨(qǐ)戟。
紧接着又派杜诗出京去，
驰骋沙场诛叛逆。

各地叛军诛平后，
又把成皋来治理。
不久后，调任南阳做太守，
更是煌煌有政绩。
他曾经广拓农田修农具，
为百姓除暴安良谋福利。
光武帝了解情况后，
又要给杜诗升官职。
杜诗却认为做官本分该如此，
还要求降到小郡去任职，
说自己“才能只够做小官，
赶上了国家缺人才把高职任。
长时期诚惶又诚恐，
更担心辜负圣主栽培意”。
越这样光武帝越信任他，
让他仍任太守职。
到后来，“诚惶诚恐”作成语，
常用作表章奏疏套用语，
表臣下敬畏皇帝的威与严，
也形容小心谨慎去处世。

Be Worried and Fearful

In the Eastern Han Dynasty(25—220A. D.) there was in Chenggao County, a magistrate named Du Shi.

About this man there were many stories. When he was young he cherished high aspirations, and fortunately he was soon promoted to the assistant royal secretary.

Then there was a general named Xiao Guang who was merciless. He mismanaged his troop and they often bullied the folk. They robbed them of their property, and even went into the countryside to prey on women. The people were irritated by their vicious acts.

Du Shi went to Xiao Guang to mention this, and tried to persuade him not to do it again. Xiao Guang, however, turned a deaf ear to him. Du Shi burst into a furious rage, and killed Xiao Guang passionately.

When announcing Xiao's crimes, the people were excited and overjoyed. When Emperor Wu, Liu Xiu was told this, he decreed a summons for Du, and gave him a promotion. Then he ordered Du to leave the capital for the battle front, and fight against the uprising rebels.

After he wiped out all the rebels, Du Shi went to reign in Chenggao. Later, he was transferred to Nanyang to be viceroy, and there he achieved a great many administrative achievements. He enlarged the cultivated land and reformed farming tools. He managed to persist with justice and do beneficial deeds for the people.

When Emperor Wu was once again informed of this, he wanted to give him another promotion. Du

Shi took it as his duty to do so, and pleaded to go down to run a small county. He said that he was not as qualified as a high ranked official. At that time the country lacked talent and he had to make a shift.

Even though he had been worrying and fearful all the time, that he might not live up to His Majesty's trust, the more he acted like this, the more Emperor Wu put trust in him. He made him the viceroy of the district.

Later on, "Be Worried and Fearful" as an idiom, is used to express a minister's respect and awe of His Majesty, as a routine way of reporting to the emperor. It also came to mean that one is very careful when doing something.

九、穿壁引光

有位古人叫匡衡，
幼年家中很贫穷。
匡衡自幼爱读书，
无奈家贫无烛灯。
邻居家中灯光亮，
匡衡便将墙捣通。
自家墙壁捣穿后，
烛光照进茅舍中。
刻苦努力把书读，
四书五经全精通。
至今提到勤学人，
人们便学古匡衡。

To Make a Hole in the Wall and Let in the Light

In ancient times there was a man named Kuang Heng, whose family was very poor when he was a child. Kuang Heng loved to read at an early age, but a poor family like his could not afford a lamp.

His neighbours had light in their room, so he drilled a hole in the wall of his house. By drilling the hole in the wall of his house, the candle light was let

into his room. Then he read conscientiously in the evening, and read through all the classical books of the Confucius School.

Even now when people try to encourage a student to study hard, they will mention Kuang Heng's drilling of a hole.

十、滴水穿石

古时候有个县令叫张咏，
一生中为官清廉两袖清风。
他最恨下属私心重，
一文钱币也要查清。
有一天他从钱库门前过，
见有人拿一枚铜钱藏袖中。
张县令罚打那人五十板，
打得他皮开肉绽叫连声：
“难道只因这一文钱，
老爷今天就要我的命？”
张县令闻听更生气，
朱笔提起批得明：
“一日偷了一个钱，
千日就是一千整！
绳软却能锯木断，
滴水穿石古语明。
库房钱币虽然多，
偷拿久了也会空。
此时就是要杀你，
儆戒那些吸血虫！”
“滴水穿石”作成语，
也比喻力小持久事成功。

Dripping Water Wears Holes in Stone

In ancient times there was a county leader by the name of Zhang Yong. He was an honest and upright official all his life. He hated those subordinates of his who were selfish and greedy. No matter how small the amount of money they had got improperly, he would make a thorough investigation of it.

One day while passing the treasure storehouse, he saw a servant put a copper coin in his sleeve. Master Zhang ordered that the servant be beaten 50 strokes.

The man was bruised and lacerated and cried out: "Is it because of this single coin that you my lord, will take my life?"

Master Zhang was even angrier when he heard this. He then wrote down these words with his scarlet pen: "If you steal one coin a day, a thousand days a thousand coins! A flexible string can saw a log in two, and dripping water wears holes in stone. These are wise old sayings. Though the treasure house has much money, you may make it empty by always stealing from it, therefore I am going to kill you."

"Dripping Water Wears Holes in Stone" as an idiom means that little things can grow into a great amount in the long run.

库

十一、东窗事发

宋时北方女真族，
势力渐强建金国。
女真生来好侵略，
经常骚扰大宋地。
渐渐地黄河流域被它占，
还继续向南吞土地。
过了淮河到长江，
大片土地被掠去。
北宋灭亡南宋立，
出了位民族英雄叫岳飞。
他当时代表主战派，
率军伐金收失地。
岳飞治军最严谨，
身先士卒有勇智。
金兵节节败退后，
岳家义军增斗志。
不料想，有个奸相叫秦桧，
主张求和搞诡计。
暗地里他与贼寇相勾结。
宋朝皇帝高宗赵构不争气，
昏庸无能信谗言，
正直之士多受气。

听说岳军节节胜，
秦桧急成热锅蚁。
这奸贼暗中传出假圣旨，
十二道金牌发得急，
把岳飞从抗金前线招回来，
却不知如何去处理。
这一天秦桧退朝回府后，
和老婆王氏拿主意。
王氏也不是好东西，
和秦桧狼狈为奸出毒计。
她说:“无毒不丈夫，
纵虎不比擒虎易。”
让秦桧给岳飞定下罪名“莫须有”，
岳飞终被毒害死。
传说那秦桧后来坐船游西湖，
得了重病老昏迷。
睡梦中遇见岳飞披长发，
义正词严把奸贼斥。
并说天宫已定罪，
秦贼即将被处死。
奸贼一梦醒来后，
周身冷汗淌淋漓。
不久一命呜呼了，
儿子秦熹也病死。
老婆王氏哭号啕，

设下道场超度奸贼父与子。
请的方士到了冥府中，
见一个鬼魂披枷戴锁是秦熹，
道士问："你父如今在何处？"
回答说秦桧也在地牢里。
那奸贼身上镣铐锁数道，
求方士回阳世给王氏夫人捎消息，
说"东窗"恶谋已败露，
叫她小心多在意。
到后来"东窗事发"作成语，
常把阴谋败露来比喻。
到今天英雄岳飞金像前，
还跪着铁铸秦桧与王氏。
忠臣代代受敬仰，
奸贼万世遭唾弃。

The Eastern Window Conspiracy Found Out

In the Northern Song Dynasty (960—1127A. D.) there was an ethnic nation called Nuzhen in the north, which became stronger and was established as Jin State. This nation was born aggressive, and every once in a while, they launched attacks on the territory of Song. By and by the Yellow River area was taken by them. They reached the Huai River and then the Yangtse River and most of the land had been occupied.

Later when the Northern Song Dynasty was overthrown and the Southern Song Dynasty (1127—1279A. D.) established, there brought forth a national hero named Yue Fei. He represented the "Fighting Party", and led an army to fight for the lost land. Yue Fei was strict with his army, and he himself was brave and wise and very active. The Jin army retreated and withdrew. The Yue army won victory after victory and were in high spirits.

Surprisingly, there was a notorious minister named Qin Hui, who wanted to make a compromise and conspire with Jin. He went hand in glove with the enemy. Emperor Gao Zong, Zhao Gou, who was also hopeless, put foolish faith in Qin's lies, and most of the righteous people were faced with trouble.

When Qin Hui heard Yue's army had won victories, he was worried like an ant in a frying pan. He secretly wrote a phony imperial decree, and sent it with the twelve urgent golden tablets, to summon back Yue Fei from the anti-Jin frontier, but he didn't know how to tackle him when Yue came back.

One day Qin Hui returned from the court conference, and consulted with his wife Wang, who was just as vicious as her husband, and often offered him villainous ideas. She said, "It goes that a man is no man when he is not an imperfect man—And it is not easier to release a tiger than catch it."

They charged Yue Fei with the "crime for naught", and persecuted him to death.

The legend goes when later Qin Hui went sailing on the West Lake, he contracted an odd illness, a very serious illness. In his nightmare, he saw Yue Fei with long hair. He furiously accused him of his treachery, and said that the heavens had decided his penalty, and would sentence him to death in no time.

When the vicious minister awaked from his nightmare, he was sweating all over. And soon after that he died. His son Qin Xi died of illness too. His wife Wang, now the widow, cried and howled and asked a Daoist to hold a ceremony to correct the villainous father and son. The legend goes that when the Daoist went to Hell, and saw Qin Xi's ghost in cuffs and chains, he asked, "where is your father now?" The ghost said, "he is now in a jail cell." The vicious man was bound with chains. He begged the Daoist to tell his wife when he returned to the earthly world. To tell her that the "Eastern Window Conspiracy" was found out about, and to tell her to look out and be careful. Later the idiom "the Eastern Window's Conspiracy Found out" came to mean that someone's conspiracy has been found out.

In front of Yue Fei's golden statue, knelt Qin Hui and his wife Wang, shaped in wrought iron. A loyal minister who was respected for generation after generation, while a vicious man was disdained for ever and ever.

十二、东施效颦(pín)

古时有个美女叫西施，
有一天正从田里往家走，
感觉身体不舒服，
就手捂着胸口皱眉头。
邻居家有个丑女叫东施，
见西施就从旁边仔细瞅，
呀！怪不得人人都夸西施美，
原来她手捂胸口还皱眉头！
嗯！打今后俺也学她那模样，
看谁个还敢笑俺东施丑！
从那起，丑女若从人前过，
就学西施手捂胸口皱眉头。
到后来弄巧成拙落笑谈，
丑丫头这样模仿更加丑。
“东施效颦”作成语，
常比喻仿美不当丑更丑。
成语中“颦”字不难认，
意思就是皱眉头。

Ugly Dong Shi Imitating Beautiful Xi Shi's Frown

In ancient China there was a beautiful girl called Xi Shi. One day she went home from the fields, because she was not feeling very well. She put her hand on her chest and knitted her brow. This caught the eye of an ugly girl by the name of Dong Shi, who lived next-door. She carefully looked at Xi Shi for quite some time. Alas, no wonder people spoke highly of Xi Shi's beauty. She put her hand on her chest and frowned! "Well, from now on I'll just follow suit, and there will be no-one laughing at me!"

Ever since then, whenever the ugly girl passed by anyone, she would put her hand on her chest and frown, and thus she became a laughing stock. An ugly girl looking this way was even uglier.

"Dong Shi imitating Xi Shi's frown" as an idiom, means an ugly one becomes uglier because of a poor imitation. The character "Pin" in the idiom takes the meaning of "frown" in Chinese.

十三、返老还童

汉朝淮南王刘安，
晚年学道想成仙。
传说他想得长生不老术，
有一天来八个老翁要求见，
都自称已经练成“不老术”，
想给他当面把术献。
刘安想他们都老成了那个样，
无非是想把我的钱财骗。
叫门人快把他们都赶走，
气呼呼地不接见。
八老翁不以为意笑了笑，
对门人说：“若不信，
待我们变给你看一看。”
眨眼间，八老翁变成了八儿童，
门人一见傻了眼。
忙进去，请出刘安观看时，
八人早已影不见。
老翁能够变儿童，
无稽之谈属荒诞；
人们把“返老还童”作成语，
常形容老年人恢复青春容光焕。

成语故事百咏

Change from an Old Man Into a Child

In the Dynasty of Han(206B. C. —220A. D.) the Lord of Huainan was Liu An. When he was old, he wanted to be an immortal. The legend goes that he wanted the gift of immortality.

One day eight old men came to see him, and they said that they had the "Art of Rejuvenation" and would like to give a demonstration of it to him. Liu An thought that as they all were so old they would try to cheat him out of his money. He then asked his men to drive the old men away, and angrily slammed the door behind them.

The eight old men laughed indifferently, and said to the janitor, "If you don't believe us, we'll show you." In a wink of time, eight old men turned into eight children, which quite astonished the janitor. The janitor then went back quickly to tell Liu An, but the eight men had already gone from sight.

The old men changing into children, was actually a conjurer's trick, but "Change from an Old Man Into a Child" was later adopted as an idiom that means to recover one's youthful vigor.

十四、覆巢之下安有完卵

《三国志·魏书》有篇《孔融传》，
有一个故事把人感：
说的是有次曹操要征南，
想早日消灭刘备和孙权。
孔融却劝他别出兵，
他哪里肯听这意见！
背地里孔融说了几句牢骚话，
不小心被他的仇人偷听见。
那人添油加醋来挑拨，
把孔融的话儿向曹操传，
说孔融一向目中无他人，
从来对曹公就看不惯。
曹操顿时生怒气，
下命令把孔融一家全开斩！
抓人时孔融家个个胆破裂，
只有两个孩子从容不迫把游戏玩。
大家都以为孩子不懂事，
有人还偷偷去哄劝。
当时孔融很难受，
也希望孩子得保全。
正当他去向官兵把情求，
两个孩子却发了言：

"父亲不要再费唇舌，
说好话又岂能放过咱？
就好比鸟窝已经摔在地，
别指望能有完整的蛋！"
俩孩子从容不迫随父去，
孔家人被曹操全杀完。
后人提起这件事，
常常唏嘘又感叹。
记下了出自孩童口中语，
叫"覆巢之下无完卵"，
久而久之作成语，
讲起旧事感慨添，
抱怨曹操心太狠，
聪颖幼童丧黄泉。
这成语，常比喻事物整体遭殃后，
个体或局部难保全。

How Can Eggs Remain Unbroken When the Nest Is Ruptured

In the book "Wei, Three Kingdoms (220—265A. D.)", there is an article "Life of Kong Rong", which tells a very impressive story.

Once Cao Cao wanted to launch an attack on the South to wipe out Liu Bei and Sun Quan as soon as possible. Kong Rong tried to dissuade him, but to him

Cao Cao promptly turned a deaf ear. Kong Rong then complained in the back streets, and someone passed this information on to Cao Cao, telling him that Kong Rong was disdaining him. Cao Cao then burst into a furious rage, and ordered Kong Rong and his whole family to be killed. Members of the family were dumbfounded when they were arrested. Only two children were playing as if nothing had happened. People thought that the children were too young to feel fear, and someone slyly went to tell them to run away.

Kong Rong was very sad, and hoped that his children would be safe and sound. Just as he tried to appeal to the officers, the two children let out this utterance: "Father, you need not try in vain. How can they let go of us if you beg them honey-mouthedly. This is just like a bird's nest being torn down. How can the eggs be safe and sound!" The two children then followed at their father's heel, and the Kongs were killed one by one. Later when people mentioned this, they sighed and lamented for quite some time. They remember the words out of the children's mouths, "How Can Eggs Remain Unbroken When the Nest Is Ruptured".

By and by this line turned into an idiom, in memory of the old things, accusing the reckless Cao Cao of killing the innocent and intelligent children.

This idiom now implies “if something is damaged on the whole, its fracture and each part are ruined as well”.

古时候，有位琴师俞伯牙，
琴技高超人人夸。
他有个好友钟子期，
真正懂琴的只有他。
伯牙若弹《高山调》，
子期说，巍巍泰山高又大；
伯牙弹的《流水曲》，
子期说，山溪流水哗啦啦。
谁料到，子期不幸因病逝，
伤心哭坏了友伯牙。
友坟前，伯牙摔坏琴一张，
好友灵前把誓发，
从此再也不弹琴，
只因人世知音乏。
这说明，人生知音最难得，
知音才吐心里话。

The Flowing Water and the High Mountains

In ancient times there was a banjo player named Yu Boya. He played so well that everybody praised him. He had a bosom friend named Zhong Ziqi, who knew every note of his music.

If Boya played a tune of high mountains, he would say that it was Mount Tai high and great; If Boya played a tune of water flowing, he would say that it was a mountain creek flowing vigorously. But it happened that Ziqi died of a deadly disease. Boya wept sadly and grieved very much. In front of his friend's tomb, he broke his banjo, and pledged that he would never play again, as he had no one in the world that could really understand him.

That means that true friends are very difficult to find, and only to the true friend can you lay bare your heart.

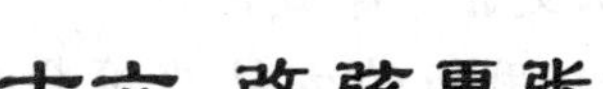

十六、改弦更张

西汉前期的董仲舒，
对孔孟学说有研究。
景帝封他为博士，
班固《汉书》记缘由。
仲舒读书很用功，
整天关在屋里头。
三年不曾出门去，
房前菜园也不瞅。
何时皇室对他才尊重？
那是在武帝刘彻即位后。
汉武帝常请他提建议，
董仲舒议论颇深透。
他认为汉朝继秦而建立，
秦朝的制度已腐朽。
这好比琴上弦索已陈旧，
不换新弦难弹奏。
施政的方针也一样，
改革不可稍停留。
琴弦该换不更换，
琴师的技巧再高也难弹奏。
应当改革不改革，
政治家想干出政绩不能够。

"改弦更张"作成语，
常比喻用新的方针政策代陈旧。
政治上的重大改革也可比，
唯改革社会才前进不退后。

Change the String on the Banjo

Dong Zhongshu, in the Western Han Dynasty (206B. C. —24A. D.), made a very good study of Confucius' and Mencius' Doctrines. Emperor Jing honoured him as a doctor, about which Bangu's "History of Han" has given accounts.

It is said that he studied very hard, and shut himself in his room day and night. For three years he had not gone out of his room, and paid no heed to the garden in front of his house. When did His Majesty honour him? Not until Emperor Wu, Liu Che had come to the throne.

Emperor Wu often asked him to give him some advice, and Dong's account was deep and of great significance. He said that Han had derived from Qin, but Qin's system had rotted through. This was just like an old banjo whose strings had worn out. You could not play it any more unless you changed the strings. An administrative policy is the same way, so you must make a reform without delay. If a banjo's strings need changing, but you won't change them,

no one can play it well, no matter how skillful a person might be. If you should reform but you won't reform, a good politician can't make any achievements even if he wants very much to do so.

"Change the Strings on the Banjo" as an idiom, usually implies a new policy has taken the place of the old one; it can also refer to a great reform in politics, and only in this way can the society make progress.

十七、狗恶酒酸

古时候有个人很会酿酒，
家里却养了条厉害的狗。
每逢有客人提壶来打酒，
那凶恶的狗就拦在门口，
龇牙咧嘴样子实在吓人，
咬不到人它就狂叫不休，
顾客大都见了恶狗就走，
这样只能卖掉很少的酒。
酒虽好由于卖掉的不多，
时间久就变得又酸又臭。
这说明险恶的环境会使人望而却步，
卖酒人应把这教训接受。
干事业做生意有相通之处，
要尽量为后来者把障碍扫除。

The Dog Bites, The Wine Sours

Once there was a man who brewed good wine, but he raised a very vicious dog at home. When a customer came with a bottle to buy the wine, the vicious dog would bark furiously to hinder their entrance. The way it showed its biting teeth was quite fearful. If it couldn't bite it would bark furiously. When the cus-

tomers saw this they ran away. So the wine he sold was only a small amount. His wine was good but he sold little. By and by the wine went sour.

This means that bad circumstances will make people withdraw. It is a lesson the wine brewer should learn, whether for work or business it is the same idea. One should try his best to pave the way for his customers.

十八、管鲍之交

春秋霸主齐桓公，
有两位大臣很有名：
一个名叫鲍叔牙，
一个名字叫管仲。
他二人之间友谊深，
一直为后人所称颂。
传说那齐襄公的儿子有两个，
父王死后兄弟便把王位争。
大公子小白二公子纠，
争王位兄弟动刀兵。
在当时鲍叔牙深得小白的信赖，
公子纠喜欢的却是管仲。
自从齐国闹内乱，
二位公子在国外观动静。
在回国抢夺王位的途中，
两兄弟在莒地交了锋。
管仲的箭儿射得准，
小白被他一箭射中了护心镜，
箭射在镜旁带钩上，
鲍叔牙连声唤“主公”，
让小白佯装受了伤，
到晚上却连夜催马赶进城。

管仲护卫公子纠，
却在途中慢慢行，
满以为小白早已死，
其实落在鲍叔牙的计谋中。
不久小白即王位，
便是那赫赫有名的齐桓公。
齐桓公派人杀死了公子纠，
同时下令囚管仲。
鲍叔牙与管仲是好友，
忙找桓公去求情，
夸管仲满腹经纶智谋多，
整军治国有才能。
劝桓公及早放了他，
用他治国早立功。
桓公说管仲本是大仇人，
放了他一箭之恨不能平。
叔牙说自古贤君无私怨，
对待臣子要宽容。
管仲他既然能效忠公子纠，
也能替主公立新功。
更何况您早想称霸中原地，
缺了管仲怕不成！
齐桓公果然听从叔牙话，
当即派叔牙去亲迎。
迎来之后以礼待，

委以重任放心用。
管仲辅佐齐桓公,
国力日益变强盛。
终于称霸于天下,
那桓公还以“仲父”称管仲。
管仲到了晚年后,
常提起鲍叔牙当年情。
他常说:“生我身的是父母,
鲍叔牙知我荐我恩义重。
既亏鲍叔牙了解我,
也亏桓公把我用。”
“管鲍之交”作成语,
常比喻知心朋友情深重。

Bosom Friends, Guan and Bao

In the Spring and Autumn Period (770—476B. C.), Duke Huan of the State of Qi was a warlord. He had two ministers in his court, one was Bao Shuya, and the other was Guan Zhong. The friendship between them was profound, and it passed down to later generations.

It is said that Duke Xiang of Qi had two sons, and they were competing for the rank of Duke. One of the sons was Xiaobai and the other was Jiu. When competing they fought tit for tat. At that time Bao

Shuya was trusted by Xiaobai, but Prince Jiu preferred Guan Zhong.

When the civil war broke out, the two princes were living abroad to observe. But on their way home to grab the duke rank, the two brothers met and fought at Ludi. Guan Zhong shot out an arrow, and Xiaobai was shot on the hook of the belt of the chest of his coat of amour.

Bao Shuya called out "Your Majesty" repeatedly, and he let Xiaobai pretend to have been wounded. In the evening he hastened their horses to the city. Meanwhile Guan Zhong was accompanying Prince Jiu, at a snail pace on the way back, thinking that Xiaobai must have been dead. Without being aware that they were actually falling into a trap.

Before long Xiaobai mounted the throne, and he later became a famous king, known as the Duke Huan of Qi. Duke Huan had prince Jiu murdered, and put his follower Guan Zhong under arrest at the same time. Bao Shuya being Guan Zhong's best friend, immediately went to Duke Huan and appealed for his friend's release. He highly praised Guan Zhong's wisdom and talent. He said he was quite at home in disciplining an army and running a country. He persuaded Duke Huan to set Guan Zhong free as soon as possible, in order that he could establish achievements in governing the country.

Duke Huan said that Guan Zhong was a sworn foe of his, if he set him free, how could he take revenge for the dreadful arrow shooting. Shuya said that a sagacious man had no personal enemies, and he should always be forgiving of his ministers. Guan Zhong had been loyal to Prince Jiu, and he may be willing to serve you. As you have already decided to govern Mid-China, you won't make it without him.

Duke Huan did accept Shuya's opinion, and he even sent Shuya to receive Guan. Duke Huan treated Guan Zhong with rites, and used him without a fig of suspicion. Later under the auspices of Guan Zhong, the country was thriving day by day. At last Duke Huan achieved his goal, and he called Guan as "Father Zhong".

When he was older, Guan Zhong constantly mentioned the friendship with Bao. He would say, "I was born by my parents, as was blissful; And I was known by Bao, that was even more blissful. Thanks to Bao's understanding of me; And thanks also to Lord Huan's trust." "Bosom friends, Guan and Bao" as an idiom, is the same as you would say David and Jonathon are best friends.

十九、管中窥豹

晋代有位书法家，
王羲之名字传天下。
他的儿子王献之，
寻常的儿童难比他。
小献之幼时见人做游戏，
常在一旁把话插，
而且句句都在理，
批评谁玩好来谁玩差。
可人家并不以为意，
都说这孩子"管中窥豹莫睬他"。
意思是小孩子只知一点点，
献之听见发了话：
"把我和那些老头儿比，
现在我当然不如他。"
是想说有朝一日长大后，
我一定争取超过他。
到后来"管中窥豹"作成语，
常比喻学识短浅眼光狭。

Look at a Leopard Through a Bamboo Tube

In the Jin Dynasty(265—420A. D.), there was a calligrapher by the name of Wang Xizhi who was very

famous. His son was Wang Xianzhi, and he was also very extraordinary. When he saw other kids play games, he would make remarks to them, and every sentence made good sense, commenting who did well and who did badly. But the kids didn't take it seriously, and they said that the child was looking at a leopard through a bamboo tube, meaning he was young and had only a glimmer of understanding.

But Xianzhi responded sharply: "If you compare me with an old man, of course I'm less smart." He meant that when he grew up, he could surely surpass them.

Later to "Look at a Leopard Through a Bamboo Tube" became an idiom that implies that someone's knowledge is little and their insight shallow.

二十、好好先生

东汉时有个司马徽，
口头语爱说“好好好”。
好事固然应称好，
坏事他也说“好好”。
有一次有人说儿子死了心悲痛，
他听后竟连说“好好好”。
他老婆从旁责怪他，
他便说“夫人之言也很好”。
像这样的口头语难改惹人厌，
生活中“好好先生”不难找。
是非曲直不分辨，
折中调和都说好。
逃避斗争无立场，
这态度必须革除掉。

Mr. Goody-Goody

In the Eastern Han Dynasty (25—220A. D.), there was a man by the name of Sima Hui. He had the habit of saying “Good, good”. Of course, for something good he could say good, but for something bad he said good-good, too.

Once someone told him that his son was dead and

he was very sad, but in reply to this he said "Good, good, good" again. His wife came to reproach him. He then said that what his wife said was good, too.

A man with platitudes like him are always disgusting, and it is not difficult to find one in daily life. Being unable to tell good from bad or right from wrong, they just sit on the fence and say good, good, avoiding dispute and having no standpoints. This attitude must be removed.

二十一、鹤立鸡群

晋朝有个人叫嵇绍，
生得仪表堂堂身材高。
晋惠帝名叫司马衷，
很喜欢嵇绍的美仪表。
更难得嵇绍最忠诚，
这一点惠帝更知晓。
只因为内部争权又夺利，
互相攻杀把矛盾闹，
晋朝的局势难安定，
惠帝时时心焦躁。
有一次，司马氏兄弟合兵来攻城，
随惠帝出兵迎战的是嵇绍。
由于众寡悬殊敌势猛，
惠帝阵中死的死来逃的逃。
只有嵇绍护惠帝，
出生入死把主保。
敌方飞箭雨点般，
数箭射中勇嵇绍。
嵇绍负伤鲜血洒，
溅了惠帝满战袍。
护主伤重身先死，
感动惠帝哭号啕。

战斗结束回去后，
惠帝难以忘嵇绍。
有人要洗去战袍血污迹，
惠帝不允还劝道：
嵇侍中耿耿忠心难忘怀，
这血染战袍要永存保。
当时有人夸嵇绍，
赞他是卓卓野鹤天下少。
鹤立鸡群鸡难比，
勇献身，当时首先推嵇绍。
到后来，“鹤立鸡群”作成语，
形容人，有出众的学问、品质或仪表。

Like a Crane Standing Among the Chickens

In the Jin Dynasty(265—420A. D.), there was a man named Ji Shao who was quite well endowed with appearances. Jin's Emperor Hui, whose name was Sima Zhong, adored Ji Shao's smartness, and Ji Shao was accordingly loyal to him, about which the emperor was quite well aware.

At that time, the court was in discord. The imperial brothers was fighting each other for the throne. The Jin Dynasty was at odds. So Emperor Hui was worried from time to time. One day, his imperial brothers became allied and attacked him. Emperor

Hui was out of the city, and Ji Shao led the fight back. Because the enemy were many and they were few, they were defeated completely. Many died and many ran away.

Only Ji Shao kept Emperor Hui company, and protected His Majesty from being hurt. The enemy's arrows were like rain, and several of them stabbed into Ji Shao's chest. Ji Shao was severely wounded and shed much blood that soaked the emperor's battle uniform.

For His Majesty, Ji Shao died a brave death. The emperor was moved and cried and howled. Then when the fighting ended, Emperor Hui could not forget Ji Shao's loyalty. When someone offered to wash the blood stains off the battle uniform, the emperor wouldn't allow it to be done: "Leave it alone and let it bear Ji Shao's loyalty, and this blood-soaked battle uniform I'll keep forever."

People then praised Ji Shao, saying that he was a great crane. A crane was standing among chickens and chickens couldn't compare with it. Talking of brave-ry, at that time only Ji Shao counted.

Because of this, "Like a Crane Standing Among the Chickens" turned into an idiom. It takes the meaning of praising someone's outstanding knowledge or moral excellency or good complexion.

二十二、涸辙之鲋

春秋时有个人叫庄周，
家贫无粮去求友。
朋友说很快有进项，
请庄周耐心地等候。
庄周一听很生气，
板着脸把一个故事讲给朋友。
说他在车辙里见了一条鲤鱼，
为活命这条鱼向他哀求，
求庄周赐给它清水一斗，
“我欣然答应了鱼的请求。
可我说马上要到南方旅游，
答应给你的水须待我回来之后。
那条鱼听了我的话非常生气，
说那样它早摆在干鱼店里头。”
说完这段寓言故事后，
庄周生气地转身就走。
庄周历来说话好绕弯子，
故事讲的道理不难猜透：
它劝人对待困窘的人，
要及时有力地援救。
假如只是嘴里答应没行动，
那简直比直接拒绝还要叫人难受。

A Carp in a Dry Rut

In the Spring and Autumn Period (770—476B. C.), there was a scholar by the name of Zhuang Zhou. He was very poor and went to his friends for help. His friend told him that he was going to have a large sum of money pretty soon, and promised to lend some more money to him if he would like to wait.

On hearing this, Zhuang Zhou was very angry. Frowning, he told his friend a story. He said that one day he saw a carp in a chariot's rut, and the carp was begging him to save his life by giving him a jar of fresh water.

"I merrily affirmed the fish's plea, but I said that I was going on a tour to the south, I'll give you much more water when I come back. On hearing my words he was quite angry. He said that he would be on the shelf of a fish store."

Having finished telling the interesting fable, Zhuang Zhou furiously turned and went away. Zhuang Zhou liked to express himself in a roundabout way, but the exact meaning of the story was quite clear. It urges people to help those who are in trouble, in a way of doing it in time and to the point. If you only promise by words without action, it is even worse than a direct refusal.

二十三、狐假虎威

有一只狐狸很狡猾，
它常想，野兽们为啥不怕它。
为什么老虎一出现，
野兽们纷纷逃散心害怕？
有一天，它看见老虎在散步，
迎上前去忙搭话：
“喂喂喂，老虎兄，
过来跟你拉拉话。”
老虎心里很纳闷儿，
小狐狸，胆子怎会这样大？
老虎本想不理睬，
狐狸却死死缠住它。
狐狸说：“从今后，老虎兄，
你别再大模大样翘尾巴！
老天爷派我来做百兽王，
就连你也在我之下。”
老虎一听很生气，
骂狐狸，吹牛撒谎说胡话，
想咬死狐狸消消气，
又恶心狐狸的臊尾巴。
狐狸说：“老虎兄，
我说这话你不信，

可跟我身后细观察！
百兽若不害怕我，
我情愿受你严处罚！”
说话间狐狸前头走，
老虎只好跟着它，
想把真相弄明白，
就连半步也不落下。
果然是，百兽一见它们到，
拼命奔逃夹尾巴。
老虎不得不相信，
狐狸果真神通大。
岂不知，狐狸是，
借着虎威显自己，
百兽怕的是老虎，
哪会害怕臊狐狸它？
这个故事变成语，
常比喻，有的人自己无本事，
总是巧借别人威势把人吓。

The Fox Takes Advantage of the Tiger's Power

Once there was a mischievous fox. He wondered why all the other beasts didn't fear him; and why they were all afraid and ran away when the tiger appeared?

One day, he saw the tiger hiking along the road. He confronted him: "Hi, my dear brother tiger, come over here, I want to have a word with you."

The tiger was quite puzzled. Such a little fox, how can he be so bold? At first the tiger didn't want to heed him. The fox, however, stuck with him and didn't let him get away. And he was saying, "From now on, my old brother tiger, put an end to your gorgeous gait and wags. God has appointed me as King of the Beasts, and even you are inferior to me!"

The tiger was angry to hear that, and he scolded the fox for his craziness. He wanted to vent his anger by biting him to death, but he failed to do so, because he disliked the terrible odor from under his tail.

The fox then said, "My old brother tiger, believe it or not, you can just follow me and wait and see, if the beasts do not fear me, I'll be willing to receive your punishment." With these words the fox stepped forward, the tiger had to follow him.

The tiger wanted to find out what the devil it was all about, so he followed the fox step by step. As a matter of fact, as soon as they saw them, fearfully the beasts ran away as fast as their feet could carry them. The tiger could do nothing but believe the fox.

Indeed he had the greatest might. Alas, how could he know the fox actually was taking advantage of the tiger's own power. What the beasts really

feared was the tiger and not the fox at all!

This story turned out to be an idiom, referring to those who have less power but cunningly borrows other's to threaten others.

二十四、虎口余生

宋朝有个人叫朱泰，
每日里上山去砍柴。
只因家庭很贫苦，
全家人生活无依赖。
朱泰对母亲很孝顺，
对妻子儿女也疼爱。
平日里尽量让母亲吃好点，
他自己和妻儿经常咽糠菜。
有一天他又像往常一样早早起，
赶进深山去砍柴，
突然间跳出一只虎，
直朝朱泰扑过来。
老虎一口咬住他，
吓得他魂魄飞天外。
朱泰昏迷不省事，
被老虎拖到山洞外。
猛然间朱泰醒过来，
拼命呼救喊声怪，
并慨叹自己身死不足惜，
老母亲无人供养难放怀，
老虎一惊被吓跑，
再也不来拖朱泰。

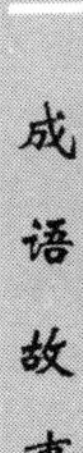

朱泰忍痛爬回家，
乡亲们闻讯全赶来，
馈赠了钱米和布帛，
表示慰问和关怀。
都说是"虎口残生造化好"，
这件事很快传播开。
朱泰他索性改名"朱虎残"，
故事被史官记下来，
流传至今作成语，
常比喻从险恶境地逃出来。
自家性命得保全，
回想起来生惊骇。

Escaping from a Tiger's Mouth

In the Song Dynasty(960—1276A. D.), there was a man named Zhu Tai, who picked up firewood in the mountains every day. This was because his family was very poor, and they lived from hand to mouth. Zhu Tai was loving to his old mother, and he was also faithful to his wife and children. In daily life he served his mother with good food. He and his wife and children often ate wild vegetables.

One day he rose early as usual, and hurried to the mountain to collect firewood. Suddenly a tiger emerged before him, and attacked him. The tiger got

him at one bite, and Zhu Tai was petrified and his spirit left him. Zhu Tai fainted away, and was dragged to the edge of the cave. All of a sudden, Zhu Tai came to, and cried in a furious manner. He shouted that if he must die, he would die and wouldn't give a fig, but he would be guilty if he left his old mother uncared for.

The tiger was terrified and ran away, without daring to eat Zhu Tai. Zhu Tai painfully crawled home, and the villagers all came to see him at the news, bringing rice and money and clothes that expressed their concerns and care. They said that it was good luck to escape from a tiger's mouth, and soon this news was spreading widely.

Zhu Tai then changed his name to Zhu Hucan meaning an escape from the tiger and this story was even noted down by historians, and then it became an idiom which means that someone has got free from a difficult situation, and what's more, though one's life was saved, he still feels scared by the afterthought.

成语故事百咏

二十五、画地为牢

西汉史学家司马迁，
祖上世代为史官。
武帝时，他的父亲去世后，
司马迁继承父志把史籍纂。
有一位大将叫李陵，
投降了匈奴在北边。
他深知李陵降敌是不得已，
替他辩护陈己见。
哪知触恼了汉武帝，
受了宫刑关牢监。
司马迁后来出了狱，
忍辱发愤把史书编。
写成了著名史书叫《史记》，
美名流芳万载传。
他给好友任安写过信，
把蒙冤入狱的心情谈。
他说道，人生自古皆有死，
可比鸿毛或泰山。
人死的意义有不同，
我不做鸿毛遭轻贱。
我受了宫刑心忧郁，
好比那老虎笼内关。

老虎摇尾乞怜为果腹，
是人画地为牢应自勉。
受耻辱隐忍苟活粪土中，
只因为先父遗愿未实现。
我要把史书写成传后世，
藏于名山死无憾。
司马迁提到“画地为牢”这成语，
本意是在地上画个大圆圈，
古时把圆圈当牢狱，
监禁囚犯在里边。
到后来“画地为牢”这成语，
常形容活动范围受局限。

To Make a Jail by Drawing a Circle on the Ground

In the Western Han Dynasty (206B. C. —24A. D.), there was an historian named Sima Qian whose forefathers were all historians. During the reign of Emperor Wu, his father died. Sima Qian resolved to take up his father's will to write history books.

At that time, there lived a general called Li Ling, who surrendered himself to the Hun in the north. Sima Qian knew it quite well that Li Ling was unwilling to have had done that. So he aired his view to defend

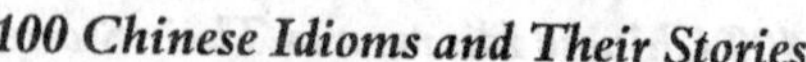

the general. This, however, threw the emperor into a furious rage, and he gave Sima Qian the castration punishment and put him in jail.

Later, when Sima Qian was released, he mentally bore the heaviest insult and made up his mind to finish composing the history book. The book he wrote was titled "Records of the Historian" which has lasted for thousands of years.

He once wrote a letter to his friend Ren An, and told him about how he had been wronged and put in prison. He stated that from ancient times, every one had a natural death, but some were lighter than a feather and some heavier than Mount Tai. People died in different ways and so they have different meanings.

"I don't want my death to be like a feather and be looked down upon. I am quite unhappy for having received the worst punishment. Like a tiger being put in a cage—the King of Beasts may have to wag his tail and beg for food. But being a man, I should draw a circle to serve for me as a prison: Bearing the insult and live among the unworthy, to fulfill my late father's great will. I must finish the historical book for the later generations, and put it in a famous mountain and then die a worthy death.

Sima Qian was referring to the idiom "to Make a Prison by Drawing a Circle on the Ground". In ancient times, a circle meant a prison in which pri-

soners were kept. Later it became an idiom, which means someone's confined to a little place.

二十六、黄粱一梦

唐朝时有位作家沈既济，
写了篇小说《枕中记》，
书中说古时邯郸的旅店里，
有个卢姓书生在叹息。
姓吕的道士听到后，
请卢生把叹息的缘故说仔细。
卢生说穷困潦倒无前途，
并非是男儿丈夫短志气。
道士说我有个枕头很神奇，
枕上它眨眼便入美梦里。
人世间荣华富贵皆可见，
若不信不妨来试试。
这时候店主人正煮黄米饭，
那卢生枕上奇枕鼾声起。
果然梦见自己做了大官享富贵，
得到的荣华富贵王侯将相也难比。
等到他荣华富贵都享够，
醒来时黄米饭未熟正在冒热气。
人们把虚幻的梦想难实现，
常以“黄粱一梦”成语比。

A Daydream Over a Pot of Millet

During the reign of the Tang Dynasty (618—907A. D.), there was a writer named Shen Jiji, who wrote a story entitled "A story of the Pillow". It was said that in ancient times in one hotel in the city of Handan, a scholar by the name of Lu was sighing, and a Daoist by the name of Lü heard him and asked him what the problem was. Scholar Lu said that he was downcast poor and had no future, though he had cherished high aspirations. The Daoist said that he had a very magical pillow, that could prompt any one into a wonderland—all fortunes and wealth on earth could be found. He could just have a try if he didn't believe it.

Meanwhile, the host of the hotel was cooking millet in a pot and Scholar Lu immediately fell asleep. True enough, he dreamed that he was appointed senior official and lived a happy life, which was no less superior than a Marquis. After he had all this to his heart's content, he woke and saw millet still steaming, not yet cooked.

When people think something is only a fancy never to be realized, they say that it is only "a Daydream Over a Pot of Millet".

二十七、鸡鸣狗盗

战国时齐国的田文人称孟尝君，
家里养着一帮人，
这些人生活开支他提供，
他们就专门侍奉孟尝君。
有一次孟尝君带他们在秦国遭囚禁，
秦昭王想暗中杀死这伙人。
此时若想得活命，
能讲情的只有一个人，
就是昭王宠爱的小老婆，
孟尝君便派人去见她。
那婆娘要送她一领狐白裘，
才能去说情保释这伙人。
孟尝君确有一领狐白裘，
可惜已献给昭王穿在身。
没有皮裘睛(qíng)等死？
孟尝君心里好烦闷。
这时候有人来到他面前，
愿替主人把忧分。
他说能潜进秦宫偷皮袄，
临走还叮咛主人放宽心。
他果然从昭王那儿偷来白狐裘，
献给秦王宠爱人。

那女人枕边几句热烘话，
秦昭王果然放了孟尝君。
孟尝君带人连夜逃出秦都去，
刚离开昭王又生后悔心。
于是就派人紧紧去追赶，
追那逃命的一伙人。
孟尝君带人逃到函谷关，
门官说不到鸡叫不开门。
孟尝君手下有人会学鸡叫，
一声声鸡鸣假胜真。
一声鸡鸣百鸡应，
守关的只好开关门。
待到昭王追兵至，
哪里还有孟尝君？
这一个"鸡鸣狗盗"老故事，
常用来，赞美那
小技能，作大用，
却往往出自卑微的人。

To Imitate the Rooster's Crow and the Dog's Snatch

During the time of the Warring States (475—221B. C.) in the State of Qi, there was a man named Tian Wen, also called Meng Changjun, who raised a group of followers. He provided them with food and

lodgings and other daily supplies and they served him whole-heartedly.

Once Meng Changjun took them to the State of Qin and they were detained there. Qin's King Zhao wanted to put them to death. At that time, the only way to be safe and sound was to ask a go-between to dissuade Zhao. It should be none other than Zhao's favourite concubine. So Meng Changjun sent one of his followers to do it. The shrewd woman extorted from them a bribe of a white fox fur coat. And only if they granted this could she do the favour. Meng did possess a fox-fur coat, but the pity was that he had already given it to King Zhao.

Did they have to wait for death without the fur coat? Deep in Meng's heart, there was a disturbing upset. Just then another of his followers came up to him, and resolved to share the bad luck. He said that he could sneak to the palace and snatch the coat.

On leaving he simply asked his master to stay at ease. As luck had it, he did get the fox-fur coat, and gave it to the king's favourite concubine. The woman whispered a few words on the pillow to King Zhao, and immediately Meng Changjun and his followers were set free.

He led his men to escape from the capital city. Later King Zhao, however, regretted the letting go of Meng and sent his guards to run after the fleeing

gang. When Meng and his followers reached Hangu Pass, the custodians said they wouldn't open the gate till roosters crowed.

One of Meng's followers could imitate the rooster's crow, "Oh, ohhhh..." it was vivid and life-like, just resembling a real one. When one rooster crowed a hundred more accorded. The gate-keepers had to open the gate. When the king's soldiers arrived there, Meng and his men were already out of sight.

This old story of imitating the rooster's crow and the dog's snatch carries an idiomatic meaning of praising those practical skills and they are usually done by some of the humble people.

二十八、假途灭虢

春秋时两个诸侯国，
一个叫虞一个叫虢(guó)。
还有个大国号称晋，
有一次发兵打虢国。
灭虢必经虞国地，
要借路须先和虞国商议妥。
虞国慑于晋国的威势，
不得已只好答应把路借。
借路本为苟安计，
哪晓得晋国无恩义？
灭虢回顺便也灭了虞。
“唇亡齿寒”要记取，
“假途灭虢”是计策。
虞国在借路之后悔莫及，
轻信了晋国铸大错。
后来把借路为名的诡计，
全称为“假途”去“灭虢”。

To Borrow a Route to Conquer the State of Guo

During the Spring and Autumn Period (770—

476B. C.), there were two very small states. One was called Yu and the other was Guo, and their neighbour was the big state Jin. The latter wanted to launch an attack at Guo, and the attack had to be made by way of the state Yu. The State of Jin persuaded Yu to borrow a route from her.

Unexpectedly Jin didn't keep its promise, and when it conquered the State of Guo, Jin destroyed the State of Yu too in passing. Guo should had remembered the proverb "When the Lips Ruptured the Teeth Are Cold". They did not know that "Borrowing a Route" was actually a scam.

The State of Yu regretted and repented after they lent the route, making a tremendous mistake by having trust in the State of Jin. Later when people referred to someone making an intrigue in the name of borrowing a route, they called it "Borrowing a Route to Conquer the State of Guo"

二十九、嗟(jiē)来之食

战国的时候有一年，
齐国发生了大饥荒。
多少人活活被饿死，
令人见了多惨伤。
有个富翁叫黔(qián)敖，
设了个粥摊在路旁，
饥荒时候作施舍，
装出笑容在脸上。
他一心想博个好名声，
好让人到处去传扬。
粥摊刚刚才设好，
有个人歪歪斜斜到摊旁，
看样已多日未吃饭，
饿得瘦脸纸样黄。
他还用袖子把脸遮。
怕人见他的窘困相，
黔敖一见这人到，
捧起食物端起汤，
“过来过来”连声唤，
脸带着一副恩赐的傲慢相。
他满以为饿汉匆匆奔过来，
会把食物狼吞虎咽吞半筐，

既会对他表谢意，
也会把他的美名扬，
谁知竟出他意料外，
那饿汉，甩下了帽子把眉毛扬，
狠狠朝他瞪一眼，
话儿冷似铁块样：
“嗟来之食谁稀罕！
瞧你那副傲慢相！
假仁假义快收起，
饿死不喝你粥汤！”
说完迈步走开去，
黔敖愣在粥摊旁，
待他追去想道歉，
那饿汉却步也不停话不讲。
心甘情愿去饿死，
不把“嗟来之食”尝。
“嗟”字本是呼唤声，
唤人来把食物尝。
施舍若带侮辱性，
人有骨气不能尝。

Hey, Hey, Food

One year during the period of Warring States (475—221B. C.), there was a famine in the State of

Song. So many people starved to death, and the scene was fearful to see. At that time there was a rich man named Qian Ao, who set up a porridge caldron by the roadside, to show his benevolent generosity with charity. With a smile on his face, he aimed to build up a good name, and letting people spread it to the far ends. Shortly after he built his porridge stall, a hungry man was staggering nearby. Obviously he was starving for quite a couple of days, and his face was as yellow as a piece of paper. He covered his face with his sleeves, fearing that he might be identified. As Qian Ao saw him coming, he soon handed over a bowl of porridge.

"Hey, hey " he called out repeatedly, showing a contemptuous complexion. He thought that the hungry man might hurry over, and devoured half of a caldron at one gulp. He also thought the hungry man might say "Thank you" to him, and help spread for him some good fame. But unexpectedly, the hungry man threw off his hat and held high his head. He glared at him with an angry gaze, and said in words that were harder than iron: "Go to hell with your hey-hey-food, look at your contemplating countenance. Do away with your fake humanity, I'd rather starve than eat your porridge!"

With these words, he walked graciously away. Qian Ao was astonished at the sight, when he tried to

go over to him to apologize. The hungry man walked silently on, and meant to fall dead by the roadside, without having a taste of the hey-hey-food.

The Chinese “Jie” means “hello, or hey without courtesy”. It is used to ask people to come to eat. If charity is an insult or contempt, a man of dignity never tastes it at all.

三十、惊弓之鸟

战国时魏国有个谋士叫更羸(yíng),
一日陪魏王去逛城。
抬头见飞过一只雁,
说不必放箭能射落。
魏王问你怎么有这本领?
更羸说大王不信请一试。
他拉开弓弦只一弹,
弓弦就“崩”的响了一声,
雁闻弦响一声叫,
落下跌个倒栽葱。
魏王连夸更羸本领高,
让他把鸟落原因来讲明。
更羸说这雁曾经受过伤,
而且伤得还很重。
创伤至今没痊愈,
我看它只是勉强能飞动,
吃力扇翅飞行慢,
飞着飞着还悲鸣。
正当它失魂落魄忍痛飞,
恰又听到弓弦声,
这时它极力想朝高处飞,
猛用力旧伤更疼痛,

忍不住一头栽下来，
并非我更羸有神功。
这故事常常比喻人，
经历过危难受过惊，
那样就遇事胆怯心虚怕，
恰如那受伤的雁儿闻响弓。

A Bird That Was Shocked at the Twang of the Bow

During the time of the Warring States (475—221B. C.) in the State of Wei, there lived a strategist named Geng Ying, who one day accompanied the King of Wei for a hike. They raised their heads and saw a wild goose flying in the sky. Geng Ying said that he could kill the bird with an empty bow. The King of Wei was wondering and asked how he could be so brilliant.

Geng Ying said to the lord that he could just wait and see. While he was speaking he pulled at his empty bow, the string of the bow made a twang. On hearing the sound the wild goose uttered a creaking scream, and fell vertically on the ground dead. The King of Wei was amazed and praised Geng Ying's master skill, and asked what was the cause of this fantastic thing.

Geng Ying explained to him that the bird had

been wounded, the wound was very serious, and it hadn't recovered yet. It could be seen to grudgingly fly, and it flew slowly and painfully. It was screaming miserably as it flew. As it lamely flapped along, it heard the twang of my bow. The bird then tried its best to fly higher. But alas, its old wound hurt terribly when it tried hard, then it eventually failed and fell down. So it is not that I had any magic spell.

This story tells us: when someone is once seriously shocked, he may be more timid than before, just like the wounded wild goose hearing the twanging bow.

三十一、精卫填海

传说古代炎帝的女儿叫女娃，
有一次她到东海边上去玩耍，
想不到她在海里戏水时，
被淹死沉在巨浪下。
女娃的灵魂含冤愤，
后来把一只鸟儿化。
变成的鸟儿叫“精卫”，
每日里鸣叫似说话。
往返于东海西山间，
衔些木块石头不算大。
这灵鸟胸藏怨愤要报复，
艰难险阻它不怕，
发誓要填平东海千顷浪，
感动得天下的生灵都钦佩它。
到后来“精卫填海”这成语，
常比喻做事坚持到底决心大。

Bird Jingwei Tring to Fill the Sea

A legend goes that the ancient Emperor Yan had a daughter called Nü Wa. One day she went to play by the East China Sea. Unfortunately when swimming,

she was drowned in the deep sea. Her spirit was so furiously angry after she died that it changed into a bird.

This bird was known as "Jingwei", and it twittered and twittered like a human being talking. The bird flew back and forth between the sea and the mountain, carrying small twigs and stones. This spiritual bird was intent on revenge, regardless of any danger and hardships by trying to fill up the deep and large sea, which impressed all the living things in the world.

Later "Jingwei Trying to Fill the Sea" became an idiom, in praise of someone who always sticks to his goal.

三十二、泾渭分明

有一条成语“泾渭分明”，
说的是两条河一浊一清，
就在那甘肃陕西两省境，
两条河汇合后清浊分明。
假如是生活中有两种事物，
两事物有特点各自不同，
便可将这条成语用，
把它们确切地加以形容。
如人们对事物有爱有恨，
又比如对某事反对或赞成，
切不可人云亦云缺乏主见，
有立场有主见才泾渭分明。

River Jing and River Wei Are Sharply Different

In Chinese there is an idiom called "River Jing and River Wei Are Sharply Different". It tells of two rivers—one is clear and the other is dusty yellow. The two rivers are respectively in Gansu and Shaanxi. It is interesting because it keeps half clear and half muddy after they merge.

When you meet two things in daily life which bear

a distinct difference, you can use the ready-made idiom to definitely describe this case.

Another instance is when you hate one thing while you love another; and when you are for something and against something else.

Try not to echo what others say and keep a dull-witted head; hold an opinion and you will be able to tell the difference.

三十三、刻舟求剑

古时候楚国有个渡江的人，
将一把名贵的宝剑背在身。
谁知他渡江时不小心，
剑落江中水流深。
这个人连忙掏出小刀儿，
在船帮儿上刻了个痕，
念叨着“我剑即从此处落”，
刻在船边记在心。
好容易船到对岸停稳后，
他才下水把剑寻。
聪明的朋友准会说，
丢剑人行为太愚蠢。
这说明做事不能太呆板，
不知变通死心眼儿笑煞人。

To Nick the Boat to Seek the Sword

In the ancient Chu State, a man one day took a ferry-boat, carrying a very precious sword with him. Unexpectedly the sword slipped from the boat, falling deep into the drifting current. This man promptly took out a knife, and made a nick on the deck of the boat, murmuring "I dropped my sword from here", and

memorizing the nick silently by heart. Anxiously he waited until the boat reached the other bank of the river, and got into the water to seek his lost sword.

You, reader, my dear friend, surely would say, it was a very foolish thing for the man who lost the sword to do. Yes, it tells people not to act mechanically. An inept person is more often than not, a laughing stock.

三十四、空前绝后

晋朝的著名画家顾恺之，
学问深、绘画好谈吐尤风趣。
时人送个外号称“三绝”，
说他是“才绝”“画绝”“性绝痴”。
南北朝梁代有个张僧繇(yáo)，
他的画艺很高名气大，
他擅长画山水人物和佛像，
不知者往往认画作真物。
武帝时兴建的许多寺院和佛塔，
里头有许多佛像是他亲手画。
传说他曾在庙壁画了四条龙，
每条龙都不把眼睛画。
朋友们劝他把龙眼给点上，
龙无眼睛不传神太可惜。
大家再三恳求下，
僧繇难拂众人意，
提起画笔点两点，
两声响，点睛的两龙破壁腾空向天去。
未点睛的两条还在墙上趴，
众人吓得四散去。
这故事虽然离奇又荒诞，
但却能说明一个道理：

僧繇所以威望高，
因他作画有好功底。
唐代也有个画家叫吴道子，
画山水画佛像有造诣，
笔法绝妙人称赞，
无人能和道子比。
传说他为玄宗画了幅嘉陵山水画，
一天内画完了山水三百里。
他还在景玄寺画了幅《地狱变相图》，
没鬼怪那阴森的气氛却也把人逼。
甚至于有人看了这幅画，
发誓永不干坏事。
三位画家成历史，
后人赞誉常提起。
顾恺之画技超前人，
张僧繇画技无人及，
吴道子成就以前不曾有，
往后也难有人超过吴道子。
后人提起画坛事，
得出了“空前绝后”这成语，
常形容某种艺术成就高，
或者是某件事物极稀奇。
独一无二最罕见，
绝非其他能相比。

A Thing Never Existed in the Past, and Will Never Happen in the Future

In the Jin Dynasty (265—420A. D.), there was a famous artist named Gu Kaizhi, who was learned and eloquent and humourous. The people called him "a man of three talents", saying he was brilliant in intelligence, in painting and in personality.

In the reign of the Liang Generation in the Southern-and-Northern Dynasty (420—589A. D.) there was an artist named Zhang Sengyao, whose fame went down to the later generations. He was especially good at painting mountains, rivers, people and the Buddha. One might have mistaken the scenery in his paintings for real things if he or she did not have insight. Inside quite a lot of temples and Buddhist pagodas set up during the reign of Emperor Wu of Han Dynasty there were many of his masterpieces.

The legend goes that he drew four dragons on the walls in a temple, but on each of the four dragons' heads he deliberately omitted the eyes. His friends asked him to add the eyes, saying that they would carry no spirit without eyes. Being asked again and again many times, Sengyao found it hard to refuse. He picked up his brush and made two strokes, and the two dragons flapped and puffed and soared into the skies. The two dragons without eyes still remained on

the wall, but the on-lookers were frightened and all ran away.

This story of course was funny and unbelievable, but it appeared to us to be a very good idea: Sengyao was literaly honoured only because he had gained a good mastery of craftsmanship.

In the Tang Dynasty there was an artist named Wu Daozi, who was also good at painting mountains, rivers and Buddhas. He also possessed an unique style, that no-one could take from him or keep abreast of. The legend goes that he drew the landscape of Jialing Mountain and water. He covered three hundred *li* in a single day. He also painted "A Altered Picture of the Hell" in the Jingxuan Temple which created a petrified atmosphere without showing a ghost. It is said that if a vicious man saw it, his resolve would never be as bad again.

The three artists became historical sages, and the later generations often remember them. Gu Kaizhi overtook his predecessors, Zhang Sengyao excelled his contemporaries, and Wu Daozi was once unprecedented, and was surely unrepeatable.

Later on when talking about something in the art circle, people use this very idiom to describe something of a great feat. Or to say that something is very rare, or when you want to say something is unique and nothing can equal to it.

三十五、滥竽充数

春秋时齐国的齐宣王，
喜欢听几百人一齐吹竽。
有一个南郭先生不会吹竽，
便混在众人中假装吹竽。
就这样他居然混了不少年，
得到的是和大家一样的待遇。
齐宣王死后儿子湣(mǐn)王即位，
这湣王和老子一样喜欢听吹竽。
可是他讨厌大家一起凑热闹，
便命令竽手们一个个单独吹奏。
南郭见自己难以再“充数”，
偷偷地溜回了宿舍卷行李。
这故事用来讽刺那混饭吃的人，
没本领总有一天难以混下去。

A Poor Yu Player in an Ensemble

During the Spring and Autumn Period (770—476B. C.) King Xuan of Qi State loved to listen to the musical instrument *yu*, and he loved to listen to an ensemble of several hundreds.

A man named Mr Nanguo who couldn't play *yu* at all, joined the band and pretended to be playing. He

thus kept playing for many many years, getting the same amount of salary just as the others.

Then King Xuan of Qi died and his son Min became king. King Min was just like his late father and loved to listen to the *yu*. But he didn't appreciate the way so many people were crowded in front of him playing, so he ordered them to play it one by one. Mr Nanguo now found it hard to get along, and covertly went to his dorm, got his baggage and sneaked away.

This story is a satire on those who want to make a living by deceitful means, for they will soon find themselves in a fix.

三十六、狼狈为奸

传说有一种野兽叫做狈，
它和那狡猾的野狼是同类，
只是它两只前腿长得短，
行动时必须趴在狼脊背。
这两个家伙常配合，
专门和人类来作对，
偷咬鸡鸭猪羊兔，
使农家各种牲畜不敢喂。
生活中常见坏人勾结干坏事，
不妨把他们比作狼和狈。
"狼狈为奸"作成语。
骂得坏人肝胆碎。

The Wolf and the Bei Are in Cahoots

It is said in one of the Chinese myths, there was an animal named *Bei*, which belonged to the family of the sly wolf. Its fore legs were shorter than its hind legs, so when it walked it had to put its fore legs on the wolf's back. The two beasts were often in collusion with each other, and deliberately ran counter to mankind, stealing their poultry and their domestic animals. The farmers thereby were afraid to raise any

birds and herds.

In real life if you see two vicious men doing a bad deed you may compare them with the wolf and the *Bei*, and take "the Wolf and the Bei Are in Cahoots" as an idiom to tongue-lash the bad guy.

三十七、屡见不鲜

西汉初有个人叫陆贾(jiǎ)，
口才好随机善应变。
以前楚汉相争时，
刘邦常把他派遣。
在诸侯之间搞联络，
陆贾十分有才干。
刘邦初定天下后，
陆贾又出使南越去规劝。
南越王果然被说服归了汉，
还赏赐了陆贾珠宝黄金好几千。
刘邦死后到孝文帝，
吕后在朝中专了权。
陆贾不愿在朝中，
干脆辞职回家园。
五个儿子都成家立业当农民，
他自己常坐车把宝剑佩身边。
游山玩水很愉快，
还带些能歌善舞的人作陪伴。
有一次他把几个儿子全喊来，
既像命令又似规劝：
“今天和你们约定好，
今后不管是哪一天，

我不管到你们谁的家，
都要住上整十天。
连随从都要招待好，
拌料喂马莫怠慢。
假如我不幸死在谁家里，
谁就能得到我的车马和宝剑。
我来往次数比较多，
你们可别有烦怨。
要是因经常打扰讨厌我，
我处置你们可莫抱怨！”
到后来“屡见不鲜”作成语，
常比喻见某种事物次数多，
渐渐觉得不稀罕。

Many Times It Happens, There Is Nothing New

In the Western Han Dynasty (206B. C. —24A. D.) there was a famous man named Lu Jia who had a silver tongue. In former times when Chu and Han were at war the Emperor Liu Bang, often sent him on missions, liaising to organize the dukes, through which he had shown his great talent of eloquence. When Emperor Liu Bang had just founded the Dynasty, Lu Jia was sent to Nanyue to persuade them to surrender. It turned out that the King of Nanyue did became

subject to the Western Han Dynasty, and even awarded Lu Jia a great amount of jewels and gold.

Following Liu Bang was Emperor Xiaowen, but Queen Lu was the actual power in the court. Lu Jia then did not want to remain in the court, and he simply resigned and went back home. His five sons had all settled in the countryside and became peasants. He himself often took the chariot and a sword with him. He took delight in climbing mountains and rowing boats, usually accompanied by singers and dancers.

Once he called up all of his sons, and in an ordering more than a cautioning tone told them: "Today I will enter into an agreement with you all. On whichever day from today on, to whomever of you I may make a visit, I'll have a ten-day stay. You are to entertain each of my train. If I should unfortunately die in one of your homes, that son could luckily keep my chariot and horses and my sword. My coming and going may happen many times. You should not feel tired and bored. If by all this you are annoyed at me, I will punish you and you are not to blame me for it."

So later "Many Times It Happens, There Is Nothing New" became an idiom which means something may occur so many times that people do not consider it at all new.

三十八、买椟(dú)还珠

古时候楚国有个卖珠的人，
珍珠都装在匣里卖。
匣子做得极漂亮，
里头的宝珠更喜人。
有一次他到郑国去卖珠，
有一个客人实在蠢，
见匣子漂亮就只买匣，
把宝珠还给了卖珠人。
这成语常用来比喻目光短浅，
取舍不当最愚蠢。

Buying the Casket and Giving Back the Pearls

In ancient times in the State of Chu, there was a man who sold pearls. And the pearls were packed and sold in caskets. The caskets were glittering and beautiful, and the pearls inside were even more so.

Once he went to the State of Zheng to sell the pearls, and came over a very foolish buyer, who found the casket beautiful. So he bought the casket and gave back the pearls.

This idiom means someone is short-sighted and tends to make a wrong choice.

三十九、盲人摸象

从前有个老国王
有一天让臣子们牵来一头象，
命几个瞎子都来摸，
摸过后，讲讲大象是啥模样。
大象刚刚才牵到，
瞎子们就走上前去摸得忙。
有一个摸到大象的长牙齿，
回答说大象简直有萝卜长；
摸到了大象耳朵的瞎子说，
大象就是个簸箕样；
有一个摸到大象脚的瞎子说，
你们的说法都荒唐，
什么簸箕和萝卜，
大象和石臼最相仿，
像舂米的石臼圆又粗，
你想搬动是妄想；
有一个瞎子摸了象背说，
你的说法也不恰当，
照我说，大象本是家用物，
我摸它，平平坦坦的像张床；
第五个瞎子忙开口，
把前四人说法否定光，

因为他摸的象尾巴，
他说，大象是粗绳一根有丈把长；
第六个瞎子也开口……
就这样，瞎子们互相争吵不相让。
实际上他们谁也没说对，
因为摸的不是整个象。
只凭主观和臆测，
得到的结论准荒唐。
"盲人摸象"作成语，常形容，
看事物片面不周详。
作出判断犯错误，
接受教训理应当。

Blind Men Size up an Elephant

Once upon a time there was an old king. One day he asked his ministers to fetch an elephant. Then he ordered a group of blind men to feel it, and tell him what the elephant was like. As soon as the elephant arrived there, the blind men all came up to it. One of them got hold of the elephant's long tusk, and he answered that the elephant was as long as a radish. The one who caught hold of one of the elephant's ears, said the elephant was like a huge dustbin. The one who had a touch of the elephant's foot, said that both of them were wrong, it was neither like a dustbin nor

a radish, it was as heavy as and more like a big grain mortar, which you could never move an inch. Another blind man put his hand on the elephant's back, and said what you called it was also wrong. As far as I can see, it is like a piece of your furniture. When I feel it, it is like a large and smooth bed.

The fifth now prompted a ready reply, denying each and every of the preceding four, because he took up the elephant's thin tail. It is none other than a rope which must be 10 feet long. The sixth one also aired his view. In this way the blind men got into a free-for-all.

Actually none of them guessed the right size, since they didn't feel the elephant's whole body. Based on subjective and groundless conclusions, one can only get ridiculous results.

We use "The Blind Men Size up the Elephant" as an idiom to describe those who have a one-sided view of something. If you unfortunately make a mistake, you are supposed to learn the lesson and become smart again.

四十、明珠暗投

西汉时刘濞(bì)被封为诸侯王，
一心要扯旗起兵反朝堂。
文学家邹阳劝他别造反，
刘濞根本不放心上。
邹阳就只好投奔梁孝王，
屈身在那里把门客当。
想不到有人嫉妒他才学，
私下里去找梁孝王，
说邹阳如何如何坏，
梁孝王急忙抓起要杀邹阳。
邹阳心里不服气，
在狱中写信给梁孝王，
信中讲世间何物最宝贵？
珠有明月珠，白璧名夜光。
但若是暗投到大路上，
人们对它也不会怎么样，
往往是见了按剑目斜视，
以为是祸祟不吉祥。
因为它被投的原因不清楚，
总认为凶多吉少心恐慌。
经常见弯木头做的车子本不好，
可是那地位显赫的人们也能看上，

这其中到底啥原因？
是由于车子周身刻花样。
刻上花纹装饰美，
谁见了心情都舒畅。
所以说献珍宝如果无人作介绍，
往往还会结怨谤。
假如有人作引荐，
枯木朽株也身价长。
可见天下的老百姓，
论本事比尧舜还高强。
论才智数得上伊尹和管仲，
还有那龙逢(páng)比干是忠良，
要效忠君王无人荐，
只得屈居下位受冤枉。
梁孝王读了邹阳的信，
马上派人请邹阳。
内心激动无法表，
让邹阳坐到尊位上。
“明珠投暗”有来历，
常比喻好东西不能派用场。
由于人们不识货，
“明珠”无缘放光芒。
也比喻有才人不能得重用，
久而久之生怨谤。
还可喻好人误入歧途中，

迷途知返理应当。

Cast Pearls Before Swine

In the Western Han Dynasty(206B. C. —24A. D.) Liu Bi was conferred feudatory king, but he was ambitious to rebel against the emperor. A man of letters, Zou Yang tried to dissuade Liu Bi, but Liu Bi turned a deaf ear to him. So Zou Yang had to go to King Xiao of Liang, and humbly be a guest there.

Unexpectedly one man envied him of his talent, and went privately to the King to heap abuse on Zou Yang. King Liang immediately ordered Zou Yang to be arrested and killed. Zou Yang didn't take it badly, and wrote a personal letter to King Liang.

In the letter, he wrote: what is the most precious thing on earth? Pearls with the bright light would be precious, but if they do not pay much heed to them, or perhaps they stared at them angrily with sword in hand, it would be considered they are ominous of bad luck. Why they were cast there was not yet known. They would feel more panic than at ease. The chariots of curve log you often see, is of course just ordinary, but the prominent people consider them to be very good. Do you know why it is so? Because the chariot was carved from head to toe. Since it was carved with beautiful patterns, everybody will take

delight in seeing it. So when dedicating a treasure without a go-between to make an introduction, it tends to be basely slandered. But if you do have a go-between, rotten wood and withered trees might turn expensive.

So you can see the daily folks, may be wiser than Emperors Yao and Shun. In history we have talented Yi Yin and Guan Zhong, and also we have the loyal Long Pang and Bi Gan. If they had not been recommended to serve their emperors, they had to remain in the inferior place and be wronged.

Having read his meaningful letter, King Xiao of Liang sent an invitation to Zou Yang right away. The King was so impressed that he made Zou sit in the most honorable chair.

"Cast Pearls Before Swine" has its story, and it means something treasured is not always put to the right use. Because of people's ignorance, the Bright Pearls have got no chance to glitter. This idiom implies a talented man being long neglected, may nurture irritation and indignation. And it can also refer to a good person who falls awry by mistake, and who should turn around from it as quick as possible.

四十一、名落孙山

有位古人叫孙山，
攻读诗书是秀才。
说话幽默又风趣，
人称他是滑稽才。
一次他到京城去赶考，
乡邻托事详交代：
“他孙大哥，把俺儿也带去，
考个举人多光彩！”
想不到邻居的儿子未考中，
孙山才考个榜末才，
回乡之后邻居问：
“俺家孩子可得彩？”
孙山说：“解（jiè）名尽处是孙山，
贤郎更落孙山外。”
“名落孙山”作成语，
常比喻考试落第未取的才。

Fall Behind Sun Shan

There was an ancient man named Sun Shan, who was a scholar who indulged himself in literature. When he spoke he cast a shadow of humour and com-

edy, so people called him Sun Shan the Comedian. Once he went to the capital to sit for the imperial exam, and one of his neighbours asked him a favour.

"Brother Sun, would you take my son with you? It would be honorable if he happened to be enrolled as an imperial scholar?"

But his neighbour's son failed, while he was enrolled at the end of the list. When he went back the neighbour asked him: "Has my son passed the exam?" Sun Shan replied, "My name was listed last and your son has fallen behind me."

The idiom "Fall Behind Sun Shan" means someone has failed in an exam.

四十二、磨杵(chǔ)成针

唐朝有位诗人叫李白，
年少时贪玩读书不认真。
一天李白逃学到野外，
路见一位婆婆在磨针。
那婆婆手持一根大铁棍，
蘸溪水大青石上磨得紧。
小李白见此情景心纳闷，
问婆婆哪年才能磨成针？
李白话儿未落音，
老太太答话笑吟吟：
“天下无难事，
只怕有心人。
莫看这根铁棒粗，
磨去一分少一分。”
说完婆婆无踪影，
李白才知遇仙人。
从那后李白记住仙人话，
上学读书最用心。
后来成为大诗人，
故事流传到如今。

Grind an Iron Rod Into a Needle

In the Tang Dynasty(618—907A. D.) there was a poet named Li Bai. In his childhood he was naughty and didn't work hard on his studies. One day he played hookey out on a road and saw a granny grinding an iron rod into a needle. The old woman was holding a thick iron rod, dipped it in the water and ground it on a huge stone.

Li Bai was quite puzzled at the very sight, and asked how long would it take her to grind it into a needle. Without waiting for Li Bai's words to trail away, the granny replied with a smile: "There's nothing too hard in the world, if you put your heart into it. Although the iron rod is a bit too thick, yet as long as you grind it, it will get less and less."

With these words the old woman disappeared, and Li Bai then knew he had met a fairy. From that day on Li Bai kept in mind the granny's words, and worked on his studies whole-heartedly. Later he became a great poet, and the story is passed down to the present.

四十三、暮夜怀金

《后汉书》有篇《杨震传》，
据记载杨震做官最清廉。
他为人性情很耿直，
有一件小事可见一斑：
有一次杨震途经昌邑县，
县令是当年他举荐。
为报答老师举荐恩，
县令王密心盘算：
送点礼物给恩师吧，
要是派人去太显眼。
王密也知道恩师廉且直，
可没有表示又心不安。
终决定怀揣黄金十余斤，
亲自送去在夜间。
杨震一见很生气，
批评他怎么可以这样干！
王密说："特趁暗夜无人知。"
杨震说："脚下有地上有天。
再者还有你和我，
天、地、你、我已四知，
你揣金速回莫迟延！
若要再来说服我，

师生之谊今日断!”
王密至此愧又惭,
揣金辞师生感叹,
佩服老师廉正清,
杨震美名千古传。
“暮夜怀金”这成语,
比喻人暗中贿赂把蠢事干。

To Bestow Gold at Midnight

In the history of Later Han Dynasty there was a biography about Yang Zhen. It says that Yang Zhen was an honest and restrained officer, who had a disposition of uprightness, as can be seen from this story.

Once Yang Zhen was passing Changyi County. The magistrate of the county had been promoted by him. In order to pay the credit of his promotion, the magistrate Wang Mi was racking his brains to find a way to have someone send him some presents.

Wang Mi knew very well this blissful teacher was honest and upright, but he would feel upset lest he rewarded him a little. So he decided to bestow on him a lump of gold weighing 5 kilograms, and take it in person in the middle of the night.

Yang Zhen was very angry at the sight of it and gave him a very strong rebuke! Wang Mi said, “At

midnight no one knows." Yang Zhen said, "but the Earth underfoot and Heaven overhead, and what is more, you and me—Earth, Heaven, you and me four persons know the secret. Go back to your place with the gold and don't delay. If you try to make me accept it one more time there will be no teacher and disciple any more!"

Then Wang Mi was ashamed and defaced like a stricken devil. He emotionally bade his teacher good-night with the gold, admiring his teacher's virtue even more.

Thus the good name of Yang Zhen goes on and on, but the idiom "To Bestow Gold at Midnight" takes the meaning of some sly vicious bribery.

四十四、南柯一梦

传说有个古人叫淳于棼(fén),
一天靠着棵古槐把觉睡。
他梦见了一个地方叫槐安国,
槐安国有一个南柯郡。
他做上了太守时运好,
又被那槐安国公主招了亲。
可后来他领兵打仗总失败,
被罢官驸马心中添烦闷。
醒来后发现槐安国是个蚂蚁洞,
南柯郡是古槐一枝朝南伸。
淳于棼南柯一梦空欢喜,
这故事讽刺那专做美梦的人,
荣华富贵皆虚影,
奉劝世人莫贪心。

A Nanke Dream

Legend has it that there was an ancient man named Chun Yufen, who one day leaned against an old locust tree and fell asleep. He dreamed he was in a place called the Kingdom of Huai'an. In the Kingdom there was a Nanke County, and there he luckily became an imperial inspector, and became husband

of the princess.

Later he consequently failed in commanding an army. He felt discouraged when he was deprived of his post, and woke up to find Huai'an Kingdom was but an ants cavity, and Nanke County was only a branch of the old locust tree spreading southward. Chun Yufen's Nanke dream was but a fruitless hope.

This story was a satire on those who like day-dreaming. High position and great wealth are like floating clouds, one would be well advised not to be too overcast by gusto.

四十五、囊萤照读

古时候有个书生叫车胤(yìn),
青年时家庭极苦贫。
车胤从小就爱读书,
买不起灯油生郁闷。
到夏天他捉了许多萤火虫,
装进了纱袋把口扎紧。
萤火虫光亮虽微弱,
也能照亮儿读诗文。
这样的苦学精神人称赞,
新时代读书条件胜古人,
雪亮的电灯照耀下,
朋友们怎能不发奋!
假若是虚度青春好年华,
对不起国家和亲人。

To Read with the Light of Fireflies

In ancient times there was a scholar named Che Yin. Che Yin loved to read from an early age, but what troubled him was that his family couldn't afford an oil lamp.

In summer he caught many fireflies and he tied them up inside a gauze bag. Dim as the fireflies' light

was, it did supply the light for his reading. People as keen as him at their studies are highly praised.

We have better conditions nowadays-under electric bright lights, why not study hard my young friends? If you trifle away your youth, you'll not live up to the motherland and your folks.

四十六、牛角挂书

《新唐书》里有篇《李密传》，
风趣的故事有一段，
说的是隋末辽东有一人，
名叫李密很能干。
他年轻时在皇室做侍卫，
办事情机智又果敢。
想不到隋炀帝说他不老实，
下旨把他的差事免。
李密一点也不懊丧，
回家发奋把书念。
一次李密骑牛出门去，
把一部《汉书》挂在牛角边，
一边赶路一边读，
被宰相杨素巧遇见。
杨素心中暗称奇，
坐车慢慢跟后边，
问清了读书少年是李密，
走近亲切把话谈，
看出了李密不是平庸辈，
回家后唤来儿子杨玄感，
告诉他李密的才气与学识，
要儿子经常去找李密玩。

从那后两个少年成好友，
砥行砺志把学问钻。
到后来觉察隋朝已腐败，
及时起兵把隋反。
杨玄感拜了李密做军师，
李密帮他出谋划策夺江山。
谁想关键时玄感未从李密计，
兵败身亡后果惨。
李密无处把身存，
投靠了瓦岗寨义军仍造反。
到后来当上一名大首领，
燃得那农民起义火燎原，
沉重地打击了统治者，
英名代代往后传。
“牛角挂书”这成语，
比喻人勤奋读书肯钻研。

Hang a Book on a Cow's Horn

In the "New History of Tang Dynasty" there was a biography of Li Mi. It was a very interesting story. It said that a man in the last reign of Sui Dynasty (581—618A. D.) in Liaodong Peninsular, by the name of Li Mi who was quite able. As a young man he served as a bodyguard in the court, where he proved to be witty and brave. But unfortunately Emperor

Yang of Sui said he was dishonest, and ordered an end to his post. Young Li Mi, however, was not discouraged, and indulged in reading when he was back home.

One day, Li Mi went out of his village on cowback, hanging the "History of Han" on the horn of the cow. He was reading while travelling. It happened the prime minister Yang Su caught sight of this. Yang Su was amazed at the young lad, and followed him slowly in his imperial wagon. He was told that the lad's name was Li Mi, and approached him to talk to him. He found out Li Mi was not a nobody, and hurried home to call up his son Yang Xuangan. He told his son that Li Mi was talented and knowledgeable, and asked his son to frequent his place.

Later on the two young men became good friends and together they established and whetted their conducts and studies endlessly. Later on they found the Sui Dynasty tended to decay, so they organized an army and rose up against it without delay.

Yang Xuangan made Li Mi his military consultant, and Li Mi helped Yang Xuangan decide strategy to fight for the country. But in a key battle he didn't follow Li Mi's idea, and Xuangan got killed and his men all defeated.

Li Mi had nowhere to dwell, and had to join the Wagang village volunteers to rebel. Later he became a

chief commander of a peasants uprising force, which heavily tore the foundation of the imperial rulers, and his heroism goes down from generation to generation.

You can use "Hang a Book on a Cow's Horn" as an idiom to praise a person who studies very hard.

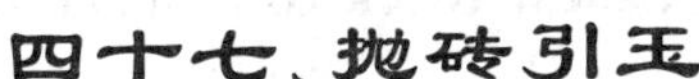

四十七、抛砖引玉

在唐代有位诗人叫常建，
一次好友赵嘏(gǔ)要来苏州玩，
苏州城有一处名胜叫灵岩寺，
他估计赵嘏准到那儿玩。
他先在寺前写下两句诗，
心中想赵嘏一到准看见。
果然是赵嘏来到古寺前，
见到了诗句随口念，
总觉得只有两句不成诗，
补上两句才完全。
赵嘏提笔补诗句，
两旁观者齐称赞。
“写得好！”声音最响是哪个？
人群中走出诗友是常建。
自称是抛砖为引赵嘏玉，
一时诗林传美谈。
到后来常用这成语，
比喻自己对某事的看法是浅见。
若想引人发高论，
抛出愚拙得高见。
“抛砖引玉”表谦虚，
而自夸往往惹得人憎嫌。

To Cast a Brick to Attract Jade

In the Tang Dynasty(618—907A. D.) there was a poet named Chang Jian. One day his best friend Zhao Gu went to Suzhou for a tour, and in the city of Suzhou there was a place of interest called Lingyan Temple. He figured Zhao Gu must be going to visit there. So he went there before hand and wrote two lines of poetry on the front wall, thinking that Zhao Gu would surely notice it.

It happened that Zhao Gu arrived at the place, and read the lines randomly. He considered this not to be a complete poem with only two lines, and another two lines should be added to it.

Zhao Gu picked up his brush and completed the poem. The onlookers praised it highly in chorus. "Well written!" whose voice was so loud? The man coming out of the crowd was his poem-pal Chang Jian. He put it that he was casting a brick to attract Zhao's jade, and for a time this remained a beautiful story .

Later on this idiom was put into common use, implying that your own view is but a shallow one. If you want to attract other people's valuable opinions, you offer him some common place comments. "Cast a Brick to Attract Jade" shows you are modest, and that self-exaggeration may cause annoyance.

四十八、赔了夫人又折兵

三国时刘备曾依孔明计，
向东吴借荆州作为立足地，
到后来得了西蜀土，
魏蜀吴鼎足之势才确立。
东吴的孙权和周瑜，
君臣共同拿主意，
都认为荆州被借已数载，
刘备已有了根据地，
西蜀必须还荆州，
不还就是无信义。
东吴就几次三番派人讨，
刘备却心中实在难舍弃。
东吴一时无办法，
再召群臣来商议。
定计谋谎称孙权有一妹，
打算招刘备做女婿。
联姻后齐心协力抗曹操，
团结一致来对敌。
待把那刘备骗到东吴后，
便扣下刘备作人质。
假若是西蜀不把荆州还，
他刘备休想再回去！

诸葛亮得悉东吴要招婿，
心中想，准是东吴耍诡计。
好孔明足智多谋名不虚，
让刘备按他的计策去行事。
到东吴居然娶了孙小姐，
又巧妙地逃回西蜀去。
那周瑜带了兵士来追赶，
诸葛亮却埋下兵将打伏击。
东吴招婿故事险，
《三国演义》记详细。
那东吴赔了夫人又折兵，
孙权周瑜气半死。
故事演化为成语，
常比喻，某人一心占便宜，
结果便宜未占到，
还蒙受双重大损失。

Losing the Princess and Bunches of Soldiers

During the period of the Three Kingdoms (220—265A. D.), Liu Bei followed Zhuge Liang's strategy, and borrowed the city of Jingzhou from the Kingdom of Wu as his military foothold. He then captured the area of Shu and finally formed the layout of the Three Kingdoms.

In the Kingdom of Wu, both King Sun Quan and

his consultant Zhou Yu thought it was high time that Liu Bei returned the city of Jingzhou to them. He had borrowed it for years and had already built up his own military base. The Kingdom of Shu must return Jingzhou to the Kingdom of Wu, otherwise, it would be an unfaithful thing to do.

The Kingdom of Wu sent officials several times to request for the city, but Liu Bei was reluctant to give it back. As the Kingdom of Wu had no other way out at that time, the King called the ministers together and decided to carry out an intrigue. They passed word to the Kingdom of Shu that King Sun Quan had a younger sister who wished to marry Liu Bei. With the marriage, Wu and Shu would join forces in resistance against Cao Cao wholeheartedly.

Deviously, they wished to coax Liu Bei to come to their land, and then take him hostage. If he wouldn't return the city of Jingzhou, then he would find no way to go back to his home country. When Zhuge Liang heard the news, he knew immediately it was a trick. The witty, military consultant, Zhuge Liang was really smart, and advised Liu Bei to take up his scheme.

Liu Bei eventually came to the Kingdom of Wu and married Miss Sun, cunningly making his way back to the Kingdom of Shu. Zhou Yu, military consultant of the Kingdom of Wu, led soldiers to chase Liu Bei. Yet, Zhuge Liang had already laid an ambush and at-

tacked the Wu soldiers.

The story of Liu Bei's courage to take a wife from the Kingdom of Wu was told in detail in the "Romance of the Three Kingdoms," The Kingdom of Wu lost the princess and many soldiers, by which both the King Sun Quan and the consultant Zhou Yu were nearly driven mad.

The story has evolved into an idiom, referring to those who intend to take advantage of a situation, but ultimately suffer from toil and trouble and a serious loss. This is similar to the English phrase "Throw the helve after the hatchet".

四十九、破镜重圆

南北朝时陈太子舍人名叫徐德言，
娶了那乐昌公主为妻是美满姻缘。
陈后主这个妹妹生得美，
徐德言乐极生悲思绪乱。
他相信“自古红颜多薄命”，
最害怕好夫妻中途会拆散。
公主说：“你的担心没来由，
俺也不会把你怨。
万一是今后我们真分离，
我这儿有一面镜子人各半。
分离后若要再相会，
元宵节卖镜再团圆。”
太子点头连称好，
谨将妻言记心间。
不久后果然灾难起，
邻邦之间起征战。
夫妻分镜，各人怀里揣一半。
别时互嘱不负约，
然后相别挥泪散。
到后来，隋文帝灭陈掳后主，
公主她被掳进宰相杨素深庭院。
老杨素随文帝一起平天下，

当时权势非一般。
自从得到公主后，
十分宠爱当心肝。
可是这公主从来不高兴，
时刻惦念前夫徐德言。
到后来德言也流落到京都，
元宵节专去把灯观。
拿出了珍藏的半面镜，
高声呼喊要卖大钱。
他在市上卖破镜，
一时京城作笑谈。
这话传到宰相府，
乐昌公主又是欢喜又心酸。
立派一人带破镜，
去对徐郎那半面。
德言见镜乐无比，
随手书写诗一篇。
公主见了德言诗，
立时哭成泪人般。
杨素知道这件事，
愿把二人再成全。
亲自召来徐德言，
盛情款待设酒宴。
也命公主作一诗，
于是二人得团圆。

这成语，比喻那夫妻离散又团聚，
好比那破镜得重圆。

A Broken Mirror Joined Together

In the Southern and Northern Dynasties (420—589A. D.), Prince Chen had a follower named Xu Deyan, who took Princess Lechang as his wife and it was a marriage made in heaven. Princess Lechang, Prince Chen's younger sister was a real beauty, Xu Deyan thereby was too happy to feel at ease. He believed in the saying that misfortune favours the smart, and feared husband and wife would be torn apart. The princess said, "You are worrying about nothing. In case we'll be going different ways, here, I've got a broken mirror that we each have half of. Should we meet again, one of us would be selling it on the first-month-fifteenth Lantern Festival."

Deyan nodded his approval, and carefully kept the promise at the back of his mind. Before long a hazard hit them head on. A war broke out between his and the neighbouring state. Husband and wife took the mirror halves one each and put them in their bosoms. On departure they took oaths not to break the promise, with tears welling up in their eyes.

In the end, Emperor Wen of Sui Dynasty eliminated the State of Chen and arrested the prince. The

princess had also been caught and sent to the prime minister Yang Su's dwelling. The old prime minister had followed the Emperor to fight for the throne. He then had a striking privilege over common people, since he'd taken possession of the princess. He felt delighted and kept her as his most favourite. But the princess was far from being content. She missed her former husband day and night.

Xu Deyan was then also roaming in the capital, and went to the street to see the lanterns show at the festival. He took out his half mirror and shouted to sell it, and asked for a high price. Selling a broken mirror in the broad street turned out to be quite a laughingstock. Gossip about it reached the prime minister's house. Princess Lechang was both overjoyed and sorrowful. Immediately she sent a man there taking the other half of the mirror to join with Deyan's half and make a whole.

When he saw it, Deyan was as happy as a lark in the sky, and set his hand at once to write a poem. Having read Deyan's emotional poem, the princess cried and cried like having a bath of tears. When Yang Su was informed of this matter, he resolved to help them to reconcile. He had Xu Deyan called to his house, and gave him a very warm welcome. He asked the princess to write an answering poem, and let the two again be husband and wife.

This idiom implies a split marriage can be reunited once again, just like the broken mirror matched its other half.

五十、扑朔迷离

古时候有个姑娘叫花木兰，
聪明伶俐更勇敢。
她织的布匹实在好，
家人亲邻都夸赞。
有一年外族入侵情势紧，
边境告急文书传，
朝廷下了征兵令，
不管老年与少年。
木兰父亲年已迈，
也要应征上前线。
木兰心中似火烧，
怨恨自己不是男。
小弟如今还年幼，
此事急迫怎么办？
好木兰思考一番主意定，
决定自己女扮男，
毅然代父去从军，
出生入死十三年！
身经百战军功立，
敌军闻名魂魄散。
立下功劳不受赏，
要求早日返家园。

木兰回到家中后，
脱去战袍红装换。
战友们前来探望全惊呆，
方知木兰是婵娟。
古乐府有《木兰诗》，
木兰故事记周全。
这首诗结尾几句写得好：
“雄兔脚扑朔，
雌兔眼迷离。
双兔傍地走，
安能辨我是雄雌。”
大意是，雌雄兔子虽有别，
跑动起来难分辨。
也形容事物错综复杂时，
真真假假难分辨。

Complicated and Confusing

In ancient times there was a girl named Hua Mulan, who was bright, smart and brave. She spun good cloth on the loom, and her neighbours all praised her up to the moon. One year an alien country invaded their country and the situation was very tense. The front passed to them urgent messages, and the emperor released a decree. Military conscription was levied regardless of age, old or young.

Mulan's father was an old man, and he too was supposed to go to the front. Mulan was worried in her heart, and wished she had been a boy. Her younger brother, however was too young, but what was to be done about this urgency?

Ruminating, Mulan thought hard and hit upon an idea. She decided to disguise herself as a young lad. Fearlessly she joined the army in place of her father, and fought battles bravely for thirteen years! Fought hundreds of battles and achieved hundreds of victories. The enemy was very frightened even when they heard her name. Deserving of so many awards but she refused to accept them, and would only return home as soon as possible.

When she came back home, Mulan took off the uniform and put on her girl clothing. Her comrades-in-arms came to see her, surprised to see a dyed-in-the-wool young lady. In the old "Yuefu Ballads" there was a Song of Mulan, which records in detail the stories of this heroine.

In the end we have these well-written words: "The he-hare's feet were galloping, the she-hare's eyes were bewildering. When the two were running along together, how could you tell whether it was a male or a female?" By this it meant that though the hare was divided into two sexes, you just can't tell when it is at a considerable distance.

The idiom "Complicated and Confusing" can also mean something was so sophisticated that you can't tell whether it's genuine or fake.

五十一、七步之才

三国时，魏武帝曹操有二子，
名叫曹丕与曹植。
兄弟二人皆有才，
可曹丕生性好妒忌。
自从他即位做了魏文帝，
更容不下曹植小弟弟。
只因为，曹植文才比他好，
曹丕心里不服气。
有一天，他把曹植喊进宫，
命曹植，
七步要作成一首诗。
这首诗，
咏的应是手足情，
作不出，
马上处死不客气。
曹植马上意识到，
哥哥要借故害弟弟！
曹植才思真敏捷，
举步开口便吟诗：
“煮豆持作羹（gēng），
漉菽（lùshū）以为汁。
萁（qī）在釜（fǔ）下燃，

豆在釜中泣。
本是同根生，
相煎何太急！"
意思是：
拿些豆子煮羹汤，
要把豆子熬出汁。
豆秸锅下熊熊燃，
豆在锅里直哭泣。
本来是同根所生亲骨肉，
相互煎熬太急又何必！
这诗比喻最通俗，
揭穿曹丕恶用意。
曹丕他听后脊背冒冷汗，
又羞又愧又着急。
"七步之才"成典故，
"煮豆燃萁"作成语，
一方面，说明曹植文思好，
也表明，曹丕在处理手足关系上，
的确太不合情理。

The Seven-Pace Talent

During the period of the Three Kingdoms (220—265A. D.), Emperor Wu of Wei, Cao Cao had two sons. One was named Cao Pi and the other Cao Zhi.

The two brothers were both talented, only the elder brother Cao Pi had a jealous temperament. After he was crowned Emperor Wen of Wei, he included his younger brother Cao Zhi no longer, because Cao Zhi was more talented in literature than he. Cao Pi just would not let him go his own course.

One day, Cao Zhi was called to the court, and was made to compose a poem within seven paces. The topic was about the friendship between brothers. If he failed, Cao Zhi should be put to death without mercy. Cao Zhi instantly smelled the malice. His brother wanted it to be an excuse to kill him. Cao Zhi was a real talent, and he started to compose as he started to pace: "Boil the soy beans, You intended to cook congee, Under the pot the stalk is burning merrily, Inside the pot the beans are crying: We were originally born of the same root, Why heat me so furiously?"

This poem has a plain metaphor, laying bare Cao Pi's malignant intention. On hearing it, Cao Pi was sweating all over his back, and felt ashamed, regretful and nervous.

Seven-pace talent was the idiomatic story, and boiling beans with its stalks is also an idiom. On the one hand, it shows Cao Zhi had an excellent literary talent, and on the other hand, it also condemns Cao Pi's mercilessness about his fraternal relationship.

五十二、七擒七纵

三国时，诸葛亮辅佐刘备打天下，
南征北战功劳大。
有一次，他到云南平战乱，
有个孟获不服他。
诸葛亮一连七次把他擒，
心未服，又一连七次放了他。
到后来，孟获才真服诸葛亮，
钦佩孔明本领大。
这说明，对敌人，
要有收有放巧控制，
心服才算制服他。

Seven Times Caught-Seven Times Released

During the reign of the Three Kingdoms (220—265A. D.), Zhuge Liang helped Liu Bei fight for political power. They fought their way south and north and achieved great victories. Once Zhuge went to Yunnan to fight against the rebels. The chief of the rebels named Meng Huo wasn't converted. Zhuge Liang caught him seven successive times, and seven successive times Zhuge set him free.

At last Meng Huo was subjected to Zhuge, and he

admired Zhuge Liang's capability. This illustrated, to his enemy, that you should be in the position of catching and releasing them freely, and you won't beat him until you win his heart.

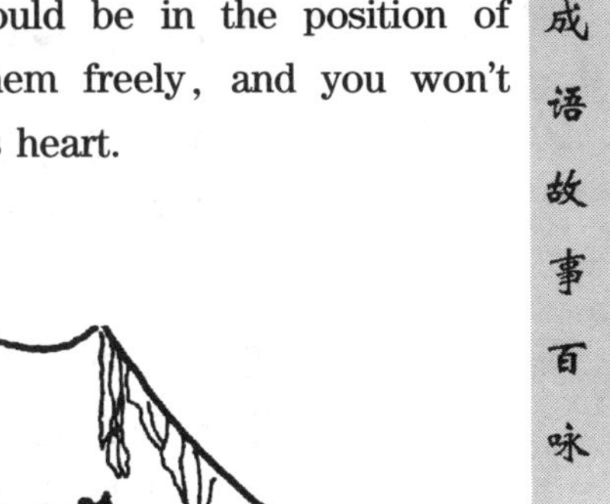

五十三、杞(qǐ)人忧天

从前楚国有个人，
他整天忧愁眉不展，
老担心头上青天会坠落，
更害怕脚底大地会塌陷。
他饭不想吃觉难睡，
朋友见状很纳闷。
问清原因开导他，
叫他不必生愁烦，
对他讲头上青天是大气，
脚下大地土石连。
日月星辰不会掉，
大地无边不塌陷。
不必为此生烦恼，
人生在世应乐观。
这人听后开了窍，
朋友心中也喜欢。
“杞人忧天”无道理，
空生忧愁是愚憨。

The Man of Qi Fears the Falling of Sky

Once there was a man in the State of Qi, who

was always knitting his brows and was nervous. He was worrying that the sky might fall, and he was worrying the earth might subside.

He didn't feel like eating and couldn't manage to sleep, and their friends were all puzzled when they knew it. When they found out what the cause was, they told him not to worry any more, saying that the blue sky was but the atmosphere, and the earth beneath our feet was soil and stone joined together; the sun, the moon and the stars would never fall, and the boundless ground would never dent.

There was no need to be troubled about such things. One should be optimistic about life and about the world. The man now understood and became wiser, and his friends were all delighted. It makes no sense for the man of Qi to fear the sky falling, and it's a folly to worry oneself about nothing at all.

五十四、前倨后恭

战国时洛阳城内有户人家，
这天门上大红灯笼高高挂，
酒宴上山珍海味摆齐全，
安排了几班乐手吹又打。
原来被迎接的那人叫苏秦，
他一年之前离开家。
这次他经过家乡到楚国去，
从赵国带来了许多随从和车马。
途中路过洛阳地，
他先把口信捎到家。
父母闻听儿子要回来，
带媳妇走出城门迎接他。
迎出城门三十里，
才见苏秦车与马。
苏秦妻只能从侧面看苏秦，
只能从侧面听苏秦话。
最可笑要算苏秦的老嫂子，
她跪在地上像蛇爬。
爬到了苏秦面前拜几拜，
连声说："好兄弟，嫂嫂有罪最该打！"
苏秦他坐在车上慢开言：
"好嫂子，今天你这样像个啥？

以前你傲慢又无礼，
只差未把我饿杀。
今天你装出了这般低三下四样，
怎不怕路人见了要笑话？
请起，请起，快请起。
过去的事就让它过去吧！”
嫂嫂低头嗫嗫嚅嚅声不大：
“好兄弟，只因你已经大富贵，
有钱有势叫人怕！”
苏秦闻听此言感慨生，
心中想：势利二字作用大！
想当初，父母拿我当贱坯，
而今天，人人见我都害怕。
苏秦的感慨有原因，
一辈子也不会忘记它：
春秋战国那时候，
战乱频仍危害大。
苏秦曾亲赴秦国劝秦王，
派兵去把六国打，
秦王不听他建议，
他盘缠花光转回家。
脚蹬草鞋穿破袄，
活脱是个穷叫花，
穷困潦倒多难堪，
家里头，见状无人瞧起他。

进门时妻子正织布，
眼睛瞅都不瞅他。
父母见儿子回来了，
根本不与他搭话。
尤其是嫂子最凶恶，
吃饭的时候都不喊他。
只因为苏秦离家出走时，
曾对家人说大话，
他说到秦国见秦王，
帮助秦王平天下。
啥时候佩了相印乘高车，
富贵了再回家来见爹妈。
苏秦是卖了田产出门的，
如今落魄回到家，
家人对他就如此，
亲朋四邻更是差。
都说他是个无用人，
这话刺激实在大。
打那后苏秦丝毫不消沉，
决心反而更加大！
他苦读诗书下工夫，
细密思考看天下。
夜间疲累瞌睡时，
用锥子狠把大腿扎。
终于文章学满腹，

能把天下大事察。
胸中主意拿定后，
苏秦二次离开家。
他先到赵国劝赵王，
赵王非常赏识他。
他提出，六国必须团结紧，
紧密团结力量大。
不怕秦国来侵犯，
有机会可联合起来把秦国打。
赵王听罢很高兴，
就把相印给了他，
还封苏秦为武安君，
赠给他许多车与马，
还有绸缎千匹金万两，
白璧百双更无价，
让苏秦先把五国来联络，
齐心抗秦才威力大。
苏秦他这就是到楚国去，
途经洛阳要回趟家，
才使得家人个个慕又敬，
几十里外去迎接他。
到后来，“前倨后恭”作成语，
常把那势利的眼光来描画，
苏秦虽批评了嫂嫂势利相，
实际上势利思想也侵蚀了他。

他认为人生在世贵与贱，
地位钱财作用大。
这都是封建社会旧思想，
今天可要批判它。

First Supercilious and Then Deferential

During the Warring States Period(475—221B. C.) in the city of Luoyang there lived a household. One day a red lantern was hanging over the main gate and on the banquet table all kinds of costly foods were served, and all around it several music bands were lined up playing. And all this was due to welcome home the man called Su Qin, who was away a year before he was passing his home on his way to the State of Chu, bringing with him a train of servants and a lot of horses and wagons. That he would take the route of Luoyang, was the message he sent home in advance. Hearing that their son would be back home, his parents went to the gate of the city to welcome him with their daughters-in-law.

They didn't meet Su Qin's carriage and horses, until they were 30 *li* outside the city gate. Only from one side could Qin's wife watch him and the most ridiculous thing was that elder sister-in-law of Qin's, who knelt on the ground like a snake crawling. Crawling to the front of Su Qin and paid him courtesy, and

was repeatedly saying: "My good brother, I was guilty and deserved a good beating." "My good sister-in-law, see how you are behaving today? Formerly you were proud and impudent to me, and nearly starved me to death. But today you pretended to be deferential. Fear not to be sneered at by the passers-by? Get up, get up, please get up. Let by-gones be by-gones."

His sister-in-law however did not dare to raise her head. Just kneeling there she murmured, murmured and murmured: "My good brother-in-law because you are now well off, you have money, you have power and are quite awesome."

These words set Su Qin to thinking, and he saw how snobbery worked! "In the early days, my parents regarded me as a disgrace. But at present, everyone is in awe at the sight of me." What Su Qin thought was not without reason, which could be kept in his heart all his life.

During the Spring and Autumn and Warring States Periods, wars frequently broke out and caused a great deal of hazard. Su Qin went in person to the State of Qin, and tried to persuade the King of Qin State to attack the other six states, only to find the King of Qin turned a deaf ear to him, and he had used up all his traveling expenses before he reached his home. Wearing straw sandals and worn-out cotton-padded coat,

he was more like a poor beggar, totally down-and-out, he was looked down upon when he got home.

His wife was spinning cloth when he passed through the doorway, but to him his wife turned a blind eye. His parents saw him coming back, but kept their mouths shut toward him. As the worst luck would have it, his sister-in-law was by far the worst. She refused to call him to table at dinner time. It was because when he was leaving home, Su Qin had boasted to his family, that he would go to the State of Qin, and help the King of Qin to unite the whole country, and wouldn't come back to see his parents until he had received the prime minister's seal.

Su Qin had sold his farmland and properties, and returned home a wretch, and found all his family members turned their backs on him. His neighbours and acquaintances had contempt for him even more. They said that he was a good-for-nothing, which was quite like a dagger to his heart.

Su Qin was not at all discouraged, but became more determined than ever! He worked hard at the classic prose and poetry, and thought hard to have insight about the world. When he was tired and dozing at night, he would prick his thigh with an awl. At length he became a man of letters and had an overall idea about the world.

Now Su Qin made up his mind once more, and

made his departure from his home for the second time. He now went to the State of Zhao and won over the King. The latter took delight in him. He proposed that the six states should unite, and only in unity did strength lie. The ally could stand firm against Qin State's intrusion and perhaps when time was ripe the ally could attack the State of Qin. The King of Zhao was so pleased to hear him that he offered Su Qin the prime minister's post. And also the King conferred him Duke of Wu'an and presented him with a great number of carriages and horses, plenty of silk and satin, and a big weight of gold and silver, and a hundred lumps of priceless white jades.

The King then asked Su Qin to liaise with the other five states, and form the alliance to resist the State of Qin. Su Qin would first go to the State of Chu, by way of Luoyang where his family dwelled. Such was the situation when his family members awed and respected him, going out of the city a dozen *li* to greet him.

Later on "First Supercilious and then Deferential" became an idiom, which satires those snobbish people. Though Su Qin had criticized his sister-in-law's snobbery, he himself was etched by the snobbery too. He regarded it of great moment in a lifetime to gain wealth and money and high position instead of other things. These are all feudal ideas, which should be criticized nowadays.

五十五、黔驴技穷

古时候贵州没有驴，
实在是件遗憾的事。
小毛驴能拉磨来能耕田，
赶集串亲还能骑。
拉起车来跑得快，
运草运粮多便利。
有一次，有个人要到贵州做生意，
顺便儿在船上带去了一头驴。
把毛驴儿撒在山坡上，
山上边，
老虎被吓得憋了气！
它急忙躲到树林里，
把那驴浑身上下看仔细。
突然间，
毛驴扬脖一声叫，
久久不停威无比。
老虎吓得蹿又跳，
胆裂魂飞远逃匿。
可后来老虎慢慢觉察到，
那毛驴好像也没啥了不起。
老虎想，
那家伙叫声虽大倒不可怕，

怕就怕它尥(liào)后蹄！
老虎一心要试探，
靠近轻轻撩逗驴。
毛驴一见虎来到，
心虚拼命尥后蹄。
它哪里能够踢到虎，
老虎一见心中喜，
咆哮一声扑上去，
撕开毛驴肚底皮。
接着咬断驴脖颈，
心安理得把驴肉吃。
眨眼之间肉吃净，
驴肠淋漓流一地。
毛驴没有真本领，
“黔驴技穷”遭虎欺。

The Guizhou Donkey Has Exhausted Its Tricks

In ancient times there were no donkeys in Guizhou, and it remained a pity for many years. The pretty donkeys could pull mills and ploughs, and one even could ride on its back when he went to a market fair, or paid a visit to his relatives. It ran faster when pulling a cart, as was very convenient in shipping grain and hay.

One day, a businessman went to Guizhou on an errand, taking in passing with him a little donkey on board the boat. He put the donkey at the foot of a mountain, and a tiger on top of the mountain was dreadfully afraid, hiding himself safe in the wood, and watched the monster from head to toe. All of a sudden the donkey held its head high and bellowed, for quite some time it made itself conspicuous. Petrified, the tiger took flight, tearing its spirits and body asunder and hid away. But by and by the tiger came to know, in the big-looking donkey there was nothing extraordinary.

The tiger then intended to try him out, so he managed to get near the donkey and tease him. As the donkey noticed the tiger's approach he furiously kicked his hind hoofs. But how would he be able to hit the tiger, as it was quite to the latter's heart content. The tiger let out a fearful roar, and tore open the belly of the poor donkey. Then he gnawed the donkey's throat and devoured the donkey's meat and ate his fill. In a wink the donkey's flesh was eaten up, with only the bowels and intestines left over. The poor donkey was after all a goldbrick. The donkey who exhausted its tricks was to be ruined by the tiger.

五十六、请君入瓮

唐朝时出了个女皇武则天，
她手下有两个大臣最凶残。
武则天叫他们俩掌刑狱，
枉杀的忠臣良将无法算。
他们中一个叫做来俊臣，
另一个叫周兴的更阴险。
他俩专搞逼供信，
各种酷刑都备全。
周兴说凡是受审人，
没有一个不叫冤，
只有把他处死后，
大事化小小事完。
到后来有人向则天女皇报密信，
说周兴和别人要谋反。
女皇派来俊臣去审理，
来俊臣不由犯了难。
他知道周兴很狡猾，
挖空心思打一个主意在心间。
他先派人去请周兴来赴宴，
周兴来时欣欣然。
酒席间来俊臣装作很谦虚，
问周兴怎样处理疑难案。

并且问如果犯人不招供，
应该怎样去惩办。
周兴他并不知自己被人告，
得意洋洋畅怀谈。
他说："若是犯人不招供，
你可在大瓮底下把火点，
烧得大瓮热烫人，
把犯人装进瓮里边。
囚犯即使再狡猾，
不招供的却未曾见。"
周兴的话儿未落音，
忽听来俊臣把人喊，
叫抬来一只大瓮缸，
底下及时把火点。
大瓮烧热来俊臣猛地拉下脸，
骂周兴："有人告你个混蛋想谋反！
则天陛(bì)下有命令，
叫我来审理这一案。
今天你既然教了我好办法，
这就在你的身上做试验。
大瓮现在已烧热，
不坦白请你往里钻！"
那周兴立时吓瘫痪，
叩头认罪不隐瞒。
到后来"请君入瓮"作成语，

常形容，害人者往往自己遭惩办。
坏人设下圈套，最终自己朝里钻。

Please Step Into the Vat

In the Tang Dynasty (618—907A. D.), there was an empress named Wu Zetian, two of whose ministers were ruthless. Wu Zetian asked them respectively to take charge of courts and prisons. They had killed countless innocent loyal ministers and generals. One of the two was named Lai Junchen, the other one's name was Zhou Xing. Both of them were quite tricky in obtaining confessions, and made abundant means of punishment.

Zhou Xing once said that all those being tried surely had an inclination to claim they were being wronged. So only after putting them to death could we eventually make a big thing small and a small thing nothing.

Later a confidential message was passed to the empress that Zhou Xing was to rebel against the court with others. The empress ordered Lai Junchen to take up the trial, which put the latter in a dilemma. Lai Junchen knew that Zhou was very sly, so he racked his brains to weave a strategy. First he invited Zhou Xing to his home to feast, and Zhou accepted the invitation delightedly. In the course of the feast Lai

Junchen pretended to be modest, and asked Zhou Xing to show him the efficient way of tackling those most complicated cases. He asked him, if a criminal wouldn't confess how could he make them. Zhou Xing didn't know he was being tricked, and he ecstatically talked his joyful talk. He said that if the criminal wouldn't confess, you could make a fire under a vat, and burn the vat until it was scorchingly hot. Then you would put the criminal into the vat. No matter how sly the criminal would be, no one had been seen to refuse to confess.

With these words still in the air, Lai Junchen shouted out to his assistants. He asked them to bring in a huge vat, and quickly made a fire under it. As the vat was heated Lai frowned and swore to Zhou, "Someone has charged you with being a scoundrel, having intrigue to rebel. Here Her Majesty has given me an order, asking me to try this case. Now that you have taught me the method today, I'll try it on you. The vat is heated up now, get into it if you are not willing to confess!" Zhou Xing was promptly paralyzed, kowtowed and made a confession at once.

Later the idiom "Please Step Into the Vat" was frequently used to describe a blackguard who will eventually be punished. The blackguard lays out a trap, and the blackguard steps into it himself.

五十七、曲突徙薪(xīn)

古时候有一家人，
锅灶旁边堆柴薪，
烟囱垒得粗又直，
柴束草垛堆得近。
那天家里来了客，
客人见状很担心，
劝主人，快把柴垛移开去，
别靠烟囱这么近。
烟囱最好垒个弯，
预防失火最要紧。
主人认为皮毛事，
根本没有放在心。
哪料想，一天果然失了火，
救火多亏众乡邻。
这家人宰牛摆酒表酬谢，
正席上，都是救火烧伤的人。
有人说："那次你家来客人，
曾劝你，重垒烟囱移柴薪。
失了火，因你忽略良言劝，
表酬谢，为何不请那客人？"
主人一想果在理，
赶紧去请那客人。

实际上他若早听客人话，
也免得，失火救火劳乡邻。
这说明，正确意见要采纳，
否则害己又误人。

Bend the Chimney and Remove the Fuel

In ancient times, there was a household, beside whose pot there was a stack of wood. The chimney was thick and straight, and the stack was quite near. One day a guest came to his home, and felt upset as he saw it. He suggested the host remove the stack right away, and keep it a little further away from the chimney. And the chimney should bend a little, so as to prevent it from starting a fire.

The host, however, thought it was a trifle, and didn't keep it in his mind at all. Unexpectedly, one day a fire did break out. And thanks to the folk, it was put out before it ruined the house. The householder slaughtered an ox and brought out wine to reward his helpful neighbours. On the honoured seats were all those who had extinguished the fire. One of them stood up and said, "Last time a visitor came to your home, and gave you a suggestion to rebuild the chimney and remove the fuel stack. Now you were struck by the fire merely because you neglected his golden advice. Now that you are giving thanks why

not invite that man?"

The householder thought it reasonable, and went to invite that friend of his immediately. As a matter of fact, had he listened to his friend's advice, there should not have been a fire and not have needed to trouble his neighbours. This means, a correct idea should be accepted, lest harm will be done to one and to others.

五十八、孺子可教

汉高祖刘邦有个谋士叫张良，
他的表字叫子房。
张良原是韩国人，
爱国之心非常强。
秦国吞灭六国时，
张良年轻有志向，
决心将来灭秦国，
报国仇把正义来伸张。
隔不久他结识了一位大力士，
这人行刺过秦始皇。
可惜刺杀未成功，
秦始皇画影图形逮张良，
张良隐姓又埋名，
逃到邳(pī)地去躲藏。
有一天他闲逛来到一座桥上，
见一位老者走得慌，
过桥时老者鞋子落桥下，
呼张良替他捡来快穿上。
张良见他年岁大，
捡来了鞋子跪地上，
小心替老人穿上鞋，
那老者便有笑容浮脸上，

却一句话儿没有说，
双脚抬起走得忙。
张良默默站桥头，
目送老人去远方。
过一会老人忽又返回来，
对他说：
"小伙子你真是好样儿。
孺子可教惹人爱，
五天后请你再来此桥上。"
到这天早晨天刚亮，
张良如约来桥上，
看见老人早来到，
正在生气怨张良：
"孩子啊，你与老者相约会，
迟到失礼话怎讲？
过了五天你再来，
我仍等你在桥上。"
转眼五天又过去，
张良更早来桥上，
不想那个老头儿，
又是早早立桥上。
张良又挨了一通训，
心中反而觉亮堂：
分明是老人在考验我，
我两次迟到不应当。

临别老人又相约，
五天后仍然相会在桥上。
这一次张良半夜便起身，
一溜小跑到桥上，
终于比老人早来到，
那老人掏出本古书赠张良，
劝张良若把这书读通晓，
以后便可辅帝王。
辅佐帝王建功业，
千秋万代美名扬。
说罢老人飘然去，
转眼之间天已亮。
张良俯视手中书，
《太公兵法》写得详。
张良心中细琢磨，
这件事儿不寻常。
从那后认真读兵书，
恰逢反秦起刘邦。
张良为刘邦出谋略，
屡建奇功打胜仗。
后来被封为张留侯，
后世人谁不夸赞汉张良！
“孺子可教”作成语，
意思是青年人前途无量待培养。

You Could Be Taught, Young Man

The emperor of Han, Liu Bang had a consultant named Zhang Liang, whose style name was Zi Fang. Zhang was originally from the state of Han, where they cherished strong patriotic emotions. When the State of Qin swallowed the other six states, Zhang was young and had high aspirations. He resolved to eliminate the State of Qin, and spread justice by revenging it.

By and by, he made acquaintance with an heroic man, who had tried to assassinate the emperor of Qin. It's a pity that he didn't succeed, and Emperor Qin Shihuang had his photo drawn and ordered Zhang Liang to be arrested.

Zhang Liang then had to change his name, and flee to the Pi area to hide away. One day Zhang took a walk on a bridge, and saw an old man striding hurriedly. Passing the bridge, the old man dropped one of his shoes to the dry river bed and he asked Zhang to pick it up and put it on. Zhang noticed the elder's advanced age. He picked up the shoe and knelt on the ground, and carefully put the shoe on the old man's foot. The old man then put a broad smile on his face, but uttered not even a single word, and stepped forward in his hurrying way.

Zhang silently stood at the head of the bridge, and saw the old man off for quite some distance. Af-

ter a while the old man was returning to the bridge, and he said to Zhang Liang, "Well done, my young lad, you could be taught, my dear. Come on this bridge again in five day's time."

When the fifth day dawned with rosy fingers, Zhang came on to the bridge as he had promised, but he found the old man had already arrived, and got angry when he saw Zhang.

"Oh child, you've made a date with this old man, but you came late and lost the courtesy, how do you explain? So you have to wait for another five days, then I'll be waiting for you on this bridge."

Time flew fast and soon another five days went by. Zhang came to the bridge much earlier than before, but quite beyond his expectation the old man was already standing there. Zhang so received another lesson of scolding, yet felt bright within his heart: "Apparently this elder was trying to test me, I shouldn't be late once again."

When parting, the old man made another date. They should meet on the bridge in another five days. This time Zhang Liang rose at midnight, and came jogging onto the bridge, to reach there ahead of the old man. The old man then offered Zhang Liang his classical book, and told him if he made a good study of this book, he could be qualified to assist the emperor, and his name therefore would go down for ever.

With these words the old man suddenly disappeared. When day broke, Zhang Liang looked at the book in his hands. It was titled "The Great Duke's Strategy". Zhang gave it a second thought, and decided that it was an extraordinary thing that happened. From then on he worked very hard at his studies.

At that time, up rose Liu Bang against the Dynasty of Qin, and Zhang Liang then hatched out a strategy for Liu Bang, and achieved successive victories. Later Zhang was conferred the title of a duke and was praised by later generations. "You Could Be Taught, Young Man" became an idiom. It means a youth has a bright future and can be trained well.

五十九、三顾茅庐

三国时有位鼎鼎大名的诸葛亮，
年轻时隐居在隆中的卧龙岗；
有一个人称“皇叔”的刘玄德，
怀抱着统一天下的大志向。
他曾经，三次亲到隆中去，
诚心请诸葛出山帮他忙。
诸葛亮草庐内作了《隆中对》，
“三顾”事，《三国演义》记得详。
从那时，诸葛孔明出了山，
帮刘备，几十年打了无数仗，
终于让刘备占有巴蜀地，
“鼎立”势三分天下载史章。
这说明，刘备真心求贤士，
得贤才，方能定国与安邦。
对人才必须心意诚，
要不然，谁肯为你献力量？
“三顾茅庐”作成语，
晓示志向远大者，
欲成大事必须礼贤下士心胸广。

Make Three Calls at the Thatched Cottage

During the period of the Three Kingdoms (220—265A. D.), there was a celebrity named Zhuge Liang. In his youth, he lived in seclusion in a small hilly village. A man who was called the Imperial Uncle named Liu Bei, had a goal of uniting the nation. He had called on Long Zhong three times in person, and sincerely asked Zhuge to assist him. Zhuge Liang in his thatched cottage wrote a "Long Zhong Couplet" and the "Three Calls" is recorded in detail in the "Romance of the Three Kingdoms".

Since then Zhuge went out of his village, and helped Liu win countless battles and eventually settled at the area of Ba Shu to make the "Tripod Situation" known as the "Three Kingdoms". That meant Liu Bei was eager to obtain intellect, and only the intellect could ease the turmoil.

You must be true and real to your talents, otherwise they will not serve you. It tells us a man of high aspirations, must be polite and patient to ordinary people.

六十、三过其门而不入

古时候神州大地常常发洪水，
老百姓可就遭了罪，
庄稼冲走房淹没，
住在地上天当被。
有位贤君叫大禹，
为君贤明会治水。
大禹前各朝治水的人，
常常都用堵塞法，
大禹治水用新法，
开挖河道来疏水。
大禹治水为百姓，
全心全意献真心。
他曾经三次过家门，
却来不及看望亲人们。
一心带百姓治洪水，
把百姓安危记在心。
后世人提起大禹治水事，
总赞他公而忘私好精神。
“三过其门而不入”作成语，
总是褒扬那些忘我为民的做官人。

Three Times Passes His Home Without Going Into It

In ancient times in China floods often occurred. The folk were vulnerable to be victims. The crops were washed away and houses ruptured, so they had to sleep on the ground covered with heaven.

There was a sage named Dayu, who was a wise emperor and able to tame floods. Before him people used the method of blocking, but Dayu dispersed the water by digging rivers. He had passed his home three times, but he couldn't manage to see his family. He put his heart into the taming of floods, and kept the folk's safety in the core of his heart.

People often mention Dayu's taming of the water, and always praise him for his selflessness. "Three Times Passes His Home Without Going Into It" as an idiom however, is usually used to commend those officials who serve the people untiringly.

六十一、三令五申

春秋时期有一天，
吴国的国王正把奇景观。
京都的校兵场上旗如林，
高台上，有个人正陪吴王朝下看。
台下有一二百美女站平地，
每个人手执一杆画戟玩。
她们都嘻嘻哈哈笑不够，
叽叽喳喳乱一团。
吴王看了眉眼笑，
旁边那人却心焦烦。
只见他，登登登下了高台梯，
来到宫女队列前，
厉声喝：
“领队的给我站出来！
刚才的号令可听见？”
两队长仍是嘻嘻笑，
“知道、知道”把头点。
“既知道，为何她们管不住？
做队长先应自己要求严！
你们俩违了军中令，
武士们！”
“有！”

"将她俩推到一边把头斩！"
"是！"
台上吴王听此言，
忙上前讲情面，
大意是：将军你善于用兵本王知道，
可今天，这两位爱妃不能斩。
请求将军快息怒，
留下美姬把寡人伴。
将军说："大王你既然命我做将帅，
军中号令要威严。
将在军，君命有所不受，
行动可有自主权！"
说罢连连把手挥，
"武士们，速将队长人头斩！"
这两个美人队长头落地，
鲜血喷出几丈远。
美女个个面如土，
舌头伸在唇外边。
忽听将军又传令，
"重新再把队长选！"
又挑出两名美人做队长，
像刚才一样再操练。
这一次，宫女个个都听令，
人人不敢有怠慢，
起、卧、转向行或止，

动作丝毫不错乱。
这将军,原是齐国军事家,
姓孙名武尊为子,
著作兵法十三篇。
吴王阖闾阅读后,
倍加赏识亲迎见。
为了试试孙武才,
也试兵法可灵验,
吴王让他训宫女,
演出上边那一段。
那两位美人队长被处死,
是因为,误将军法作笑谈。
孙武几次施号令,
如同轻风吹耳边。
三令五申不听从,
嘻嘻哈哈耍笑玩。
孙武先斩二美姬,
其他宫女吓破胆。
命令这才都遵从,
严格执行真灵验。
到后来,“三令五申”作成语,
常形容,命令告诫许多遍。
反复强调要执行,
不能马虎与迁延。

Repeatedly Give Injunctions

One day during the Spring and Autumn Period (770—476B. C.), in the State of Wu, the king was on a sightseeing tour. On the drilling ground of the capital the flags looked like a forest. On the platform, a man was keeping the king company. On the ground hundreds of fair maidens was standing, each with a carved spear in their hands. They were giggling and smiling on end, chirping there and making a great fuss.

The king watched it with a broad smile on his face, while his companion was very upset. As could be seen, he mounted the platform and came over to a row of the girls and shouted, "Come out whoever is the chief! I demand you, have you heard the order?"

The two chiefs were still smiling: "Yes, yes, we did," they were nodding. "You heard it, but why didn't you control them? As chiefs, you should be strict with yourselves! So you have violated the army regulations. Warriors there!" "Yes, sir." "Take them aside and cut off their heads!" "Yes, sir!"

When the King of Wu, standing on the platform heard this, he soon dispatched a messenger to curry favor for them. He meant to say that, "oh my dear general, you are very tactful in battles and I know that, but today you can't kill my two favourite concu-

bines." He asked the general to ease his anger and spare his beautiful concubines to keep him company.

But the general said, "Since Your Majesty has made me a general, the rules in the army must be hung on to tightly. When a general is dealing with the army, Your Majesty's decree may not be accepted. I have my own right to act!"

With these words, the general waved his hand, "Warriors, cut off the two chiefs' heads right away!" Those two beauties' heads fell on the ground. The fresh red blood sprayed a dozen yards away. The fair ladies there all turned pale and stuck their tongues out. Then they heard another order from the general "Come and re-elect new chiefs!"

Another two beauties were picked out to be chiefs, to train and to drill them as before. Up to now, the ladies had become awfully obedient. They prompted their actions without dilly-dallying, rising, lying, turning, walking and halting. They did all these without the slightest of errors. This general was none other than the strategist in the State of Qi. His name was Sun Wu and he wrote a book entitled "The Art of War", 13 chapters in all.

The King of Wu appreciated it very much after he read it, and went to see him in person. In order to test Sun Wu's talent, and to try his strategy as well, the King of Wu asked him to train the palace maids,

as we just described above.

The two beautiful chiefs were beheaded because they regarded the military law as play. After Sun Wu killed the two beautiful concubines all the palace maids were quite terrified. The orders were to be obeyed soundly and this showed that Sun's tactic worked very well.

Later "Repeatedly Give Injunctions" became an idiom which often means orders are repeated many times. The commander emphasizes the order repeatedly and that should be done quickly and without delay.

六十二、三纸无驴

从前有个读书人，
最喜欢卖弄自己有学问，
人们称他为“博士”，
可是他，听不出内含讽刺音。
有一次，他家买驴要写契约，
“博士”竟铺纸挥毫作诗文，
摇头晃脑哼唧唧，
几张素笺眨眼尽。
几张未见一“驴”字，
卖驴人，有事心急忙催问，
“你写的这些都是啥？”
博士说：“看起来，
你根本不懂诗和文。
‘驴’字马上就写到，
请你莫急坐安稳。”
到后来，“博士买驴”成笑谈，
以此嘲笑这样的人：
作文赋诗无要领，
废话连篇最气人。
离题万里谁愿读？
“三纸无驴”笑煞人。

Having Written Three Sheets of Paper Without the Donkey

There was a scholar, who liked to brag about himself. People called him doctor and he accepted it without noticing the hidden sarcasm. Once his family went to buy a donkey and a contract was to be made.

The "doctor" set his pen immediately to write a poem. He rocked his head and hummed along and several sheets of paper had been finished. Several sheets finished without mentioning one single word "donkey". The donkey-seller was busy and asked hurriedly, "What the devil are you writing?" The learned doctor said, "It seems you know nothing about poems and prose, 'donkey' will be reached soon, you just sit there and wait."

Later on, the "doctor" buying a donkey became a laughing stock, that mocks those who haven't got the gift of writing poetry and prose, but stuffs his writing with nonsense and cliche. Gliding away from the main theme, who likes to read it? And the way the "doctor" was buying a donkey was ridiculous.

六十三、塞翁失马

从前有个老人住在边塞上，
养了匹马儿真雄壮。
没想到那天马儿跑丢了，
惊动了亲戚朋友来看望，
都安慰老人莫伤心。
老人说：
“看我哪儿带伤心样？
乍一看丢马好像是坏事，
也可能灾祸背后是吉祥。”
过几天那马竟然跑回来，
还带来一匹好马在一旁。
“塞翁失马”作成语，
“安知非福”紧配上，
常比喻暂时的挫折或损失，
往往是事物的表面相。
也许坏事变好事，
其中有辩证的因素藏。

The Old Frontiersman Losing His Horse

Once upon a time, an old man lived in the frontier and raised a horse which was very very strong.

Unexpectedly one day the horse had run away, and upon hearing of it, his friends and relatives all came to see him. They consoled him not to be sad.

The old man said, "I don't feel sad at all. For losing a horse looks like a bad thing, but bad things might beget auspiciousness." A few days later the horse came back bringing a better steed with it.

"The old frontiersman losing his horse" became an idiom, and it is often followed by "How do you know it isn't a blessing?" It means some temporary difficulties and hardships may be of a phenomenal matter. And bad things may be changed into good ones. There's always something dialectical hidden in it.

六十四、少见多怪

东汉时有个文人叫牟(móu)融，
他写的《牟子》一书颇有名。
这书里有一个故事很有趣，
专把那见识短浅的人嘲讽。
说的是古代有这样一个人，
从未见骆驼长的啥身形。
有一天大路上几只骆驼在行走，
这个人看见之后很吃惊。
为什么这东西背上生疙瘩？
“是奇迹！”这人连连发喊声。
“大伙儿都快来看呀，
看这马得的是什么病！
它走路时一冲一冲多么慢，
脊背都长疮发了肿！”
大伙儿闻听哈哈笑，
对他说：“哪里是什么马背肿！
路上走的是骆驼，
脊背上长的肉瘤叫驼峰。”
又告诉他驼峰有双也有单，
沙漠人把骆驼当车用。
即使是十天半月不吃喝，
照样能在沙漠行。

载货驮人很方便，
哪里是什么马背肿！
那人一听羞得慌，
红着脸匆匆跑开不作声。
“少见多怪”作成语，
常把那见识短浅、自以为是的人嘲讽。

See Less, Wonder More

In the Han Dynasty (206B. C. —220A. D.), there was a man of letters named Mou Rong. His book "Mouzi" was very famous. There was a story in it which was very interesting, that especially satires those shallow people.

The story goes that in ancient times there lived such a man, who'd never seen what a camel looked like. One day he met some camels walking on the road, and it gave him quite a shock. Why did this thing have mounds on its back? "It's amazing" this man murmured to himself. "Come and see, everybody! Come and see what illness this horse has on its back! It is staggering, staggering, how slowly it moves. Its back is swollen and it has got a sore!"

People burst into laughter when they heard him and told him that it wasn't a horse with a swollen back, that thing walking steadily on the road was a camel. The mounds on its back were called hunches.

And they told him that camels could have single hunches or double ones, which were used by people as wagons. Even if they fast for 10 or 15 days, they could walk along just as well on the sands. They carried goods and people on their convenient backs. How could you call it a horse with a swollen back?

On hearing that, the man's face turned red and he sneaked away without a word. "See Less and Wonder More" became an idiom. It satires those who are shallow and wanton.

六十五、守株待兔

古时候有个农夫去锄田，
有一棵大树长在田中间，
忽然间一只兔子跑过来，
一头撞上大树干。
兔子立时被撞死，
农夫见了心欢喜。
他扔了锄头拎起兔，
跑回家去做晚饭。
一顿兔肉肥又美，
第二天，他早早起床又下了田。
从那后他再不愿辛劳把田锄，
躲一旁专等兔子撞树干。
田里边杂草丛生庄稼黄，
可是他兔子影儿再没见。
说起来，这个农夫太可笑，
就因他头脑太简单。
滋长了好逸恶劳坏思想，
人人骂他是懒蛋。
“守株待兔”这成语，
告诉人，真正的收获靠实干。
主观上不愿辛劳去争取，
只能是守株待兔的大懒汉。

Wait by the Stump for More Hares to Come

Once upon a time, there was a farmer who went to weed in the field. In the middle of the field stood a big tree. Suddenly a hare came running over, and dashed itself against the stump of the tree, and the hare was dead in no time. The farmer was pleased when he saw it, and threw down his hoe, picked up the hare, and ran home to roast the hare for his dinner.

The hare was meaty and delicious. The next day he ate up the rest of the hare and went to the field again. From then on he no longer liked to till the land, but just hid himself beside the tree stump and waited for more hares to bump against it. The weed then outgrew the crops and the crops became pale, but he saw no sign of hares ever after.

So we see this farmer was very ridiculous, because he was so single-minded. He nursed the idea of seeking leisure and hating labour, and every one of us call him lazybones. So this idiom "Wait by the Stump for More Hares to Come" tells us you shall reap what you have sowed. If you don't take pains to do something, you'll be just like that sluggard.

六十六、拾人牙慧

东晋时有个大学者，
他的名字叫殷浩，
爱读《老子》和《易经》，
说起话引经据典颇深奥。
他有个外甥叫韩康伯，
善于谈吐性乖巧，
殷浩开初很喜欢他，
平日里注意启发和引导。
后来殷浩带兵打仗失利被罢官，
流放后仍和外甥在一道。
有一次见外甥正对别人发议论，
细听听全是自己说过的那一套，
个人的见解没一点，
那得意样子让舅舅觉得羞又臊。
殷浩说这孩子才疏学亦浅，
却自鸣得意唱高调，
实际上他的那点知识儿，
连我耳后的灰垢(gòu)都没学到！
到后来“拾人牙慧”作成语，
常比喻说话作文老一套。
别人的东西改头换面巧抄袭，
自己的见解实在找不到。

Pick Up Others' Phrases

In the Eastern Jin Dynasty (317—420A. D.), there was a learned scholar, whose name was Yin Hao. He liked to read "Lao Zi" and "The Book of Changes". He backed up his statements with quotations and his statements usually bore good insights.

He had a nephew named Han Kangbo, who was good at talking and very cunning too. At first Yin Hao had quite a dose of liking for him, and tried often to instruct and direct him. Later, when Yin was removed from his post after he had failed to lead an army to victory, he came to live with his nephew after the exile.

One day he saw his nephew talking to people, and he found it was just what he told him. As to his own opinions he had none. His vainglory made his uncle feel shamed. Yin Hao said this silly thing was very shallow, but he blew hard and boasted all along. Actually all that he learned may be less than the dust behind my ears.

Later on "Pick Up Other's Phrases" became an idiom, and it means someone is apt to use cliches in speaking and writing, or skillfully copy what others have said. There are no viewpoints in it that can be called his own.

六十七、四面楚歌

秦二世后楚汉争，
楚霸王项羽霸难成，
后来遭困在垓下，
刘邦韩信会用兵。
先是用的激将法，
他们知项羽性急躁，
项羽果然出营来，
提枪跃马真骁勇。
无奈汉兵人马多，
杀了一层又一层，
十面埋伏难突破，
只得退回垓(gāi)下营。
项羽心中增烦恼，
借酒浇愁愁更增。
夫人虞姬善舞剑，
为他解愁助酒兴。
刘汉还有智张良，
攻心战术最精通，
便叫士兵唱楚歌，
楚营兵士动乡情。
思念父母与妻子，
不禁个个放悲声。

没有救兵和粮草，
无心恋战逃出营。
项王眼见大势去，
牵出“乌骓(zhuī)”放悲声，
虞姬舞罢自刎死，
霸王孤身朝外冲。
单骑来到乌江岸，
自觉无颜回江东。
拔出宝剑自刎时，
年纪三十刚挂零。
“四面楚歌”作成语，
常常用来比困境。
四面受敌无援时，
便可用它来形容。

Be Besieged with the Songs of Chu State on All Sides

After the reign of Qin II(210—207B. C.), there was a war between the state of Chu and the State of Han. Hegemon King of Chu, Xiang Yu could not succeed. He was besieged at Gaixia in the end, all because his opponent Liu Bang's general Han Xin had brilliant military talent. First he used the taunting method, for he knew Xiang Yu had a hot temper. Xiang Yu duly came out of the barracks, holding his

spear and spurring his horse looking really heroic.

But owing to Han state's majority of horses and soldiers' morale, though he killed one layer and another layer, the 10-li ambush he could not break. He had to withdraw to his barracks in Gaixia.

Xiang Yu was feeling reckless, and he was trying to get rid of the recklessness by drinking alcohol. His wife Yu Ji was good at comforting, and she danced for his drinking. Liu Bang had another talented general Zhang Liang. He was skilled at psycho-warfare. He ordered his soldiers to sing the songs of the Chu region and the Chu's soldiers were all drowned in nostalgia, thinking of their wives and children. They all burst into tears.

Lacking reinforcement and supplies they all played hooky and ran out of the barracks. King Xiang found himself at the end of his tether. Yu Ji then danced and killed herself. The Hegemon King dashed out on his own. Then he came to the shore of the Yangtze River and felt ashamed of going back to the eastbank of the river. He drew out his sword and committed suicide. He was then only around thirty.

"Besieged by Chu's Songs on All Sides" became an idiom, which indicates someone is in real trouble. When attacked by the enemies on all sides-this idiom can be used to express that situation.

六十八、螳臂当车

一只螳螂胆子大，
大车来了也不怕，
它高高举起两把钳，
对准车轮猛劈下。
车子高高轮巨大，
车轮滚滚朝前轧，
无奈螳臂太脆弱，
一下压成了烂泥巴。
大胆狂妄的小螳螂，
给世界留下个大笑话。
不自量力太愚蠢，
谁也不要仿效它。

A Mantis Trying to Obstruct a Chariot

A Mantis was very brave. A chariot was coming and it was not afraid. It raised its two clamps high and struck heavily against the wheel of the chariot. The chariot was high and the wheels were big, and they were rolling, rolling and heading along. Too weak, alas, were the mantis' arms, and the mantis was then crushed to dust. Rash and imprudent the mantis was though, it left the world a big laughing-

stock. Being self-important was a silly thing to do. No one would be foolish enough to follow suit.

六十九、桐叶封弟

周武王死时长子姬诵还是个小娃娃，
这姬诵虽继位却难以治国家，
就由他叔父姬旦辅佐他。
他便是周公辅佐的周成王，
太平世多亏这叔侄俩。
成王的弟弟叫姬虞，
平时和哥哥姬诵同玩耍。
有一次，姬诵捡起一片桐树叶，
剪成个圭玉的形状手里拿，
“我用这封你到唐国做君主！”
其实是小孩子说的玩笑话。
这句玩笑话刚出口，
一旁的叔叔听见啦，
到后来周公经常劝成王：
“做天子可不能说玩笑话。”
便真的封了姬虞为唐君，
那姬虞把唐地治理得真不差。
他改修良田兴水利，
提倡农耕强国家。
他死后儿子姬燮（xiè）继父业，
改唐为晋是后话。
晋水旁建起了一座庙宇叫晋祠，

后人便千秋万代纪念他父子俩。

Presents Vavasory to His Younger Brother with a Tung Leaf

When King Wu, in the Western Zhou Dynasty (1122—771B. C.) died, his eldest son Ji Yong was only a baby. Young as he was, he had to inherit his father's throne. So his uncle Ji Dan was appointed to help him, and this is called Duke Zhou aiding King Zhou Cheng.

Thanks to the uncle and nephew, the people had peaceful times. King Cheng's younger brother named Ji Yu, liked to played with him. Once, the elder brother picked up a tung leaf, and cut it into the shape of Gui-jade. "With this I confer upon you Lord of Tang State!"

Obviously, it was only a joke between the two children, but when that was said, Uncle Duke Zhou heard it and took it seriously. After that Duke Zhou often warned him: "Nothing is a joke to a king." He then duly conferred Lord of Tang State on Ji Yu, and the latter ran the state really well. He improved farming and navigation systems, and he promoted agriculture to strengthen the state's power.

When he died his son Ji Xie inherited the lordship. Who would later change the Tang into the Jin

State. Beside the Jin River a temple was built: the Jin Memorial Temple, and later generations remember the father and son for ever.

七十、望梅止渴

三国时期有一天，
曹操领兵去征战，
途中士兵皆口渴，
附近无处觅水源。
曹操心内正焦急，
忽有一计浮心田，
传令说：
“前边有片梅树林，
结的梅子甜又酸，
梅林不远马上到，
摘吃解渴又解馋。”
大家听了此令后，
个个心中都喜欢。
条件反射起作用，
顿觉口水似涌泉。
“望梅止渴”作成语，
是用想象中事物作慰安。

Quench One's Thirst by Thinking of Plums

One day during the period of the Three Kingdoms (220—265A. D.), Cao Cao led his soldiers to fight a

battle. On the way his soldiers were all feeling thirsty, but there was no water nearby. Cao Cao got worried in his heart, when suddenly an idea occurred in his mind.

Then he let his order be passed down : "There are plum trees ahead, and the plums on the trees are sweets and sour. We'll get there in no time, then you'll be plucking and eating them." When the soldiers all heard the command, they soon felt their mouths watering.

The idiom "Quench One's Thirst by Thinking of Plums" usually means to console oneself with false hopes.

七十一、危如累卵

春秋时晋国的晋灵公，
即位后一天天变昏庸。
平日里生活奢侈贪享乐，
忘记了国家和百姓。
为了自己玩得好，
这一天召集群臣下命令，
叫他们多多准备好木料，
把全国民工都调动，
为他建一座新楼台，
半年之内要完工。
他也知文武群臣会反对，
发狠说我的主意已拿定，
谁要胆敢来劝阻，
小心他立时活不成。
有一位大夫叫荀息，
既有胆略又忠诚。
他要觐见晋灵公，
灵公心里不高兴。
明知他是来劝谏，
心想荀息不要命了。
荀息他也知有危险，
见到灵公却申明：

“今天我并非来劝谏，
陪主公玩玩行不行？”
灵公一听心欢喜，
脸上立刻现笑容。
荀息拿出了九颗蛋，
十二颗棋子托手中，
说能将棋子垒起来，
再把鸡蛋放在顶。
一个一个垒上去，
“主公你一见准高兴！”
灵公想，这游戏寡人从未见，
“好好好”地夸连声。
荀息一旁定定神，
捏定棋子手轻轻，
一颗一颗朝上垒，
颗颗棋子都摆定，
又把鸡蛋朝上放，
观者人人把气屏。
灵公连说“太危险”，
荀大夫至此开口语轻轻：
“主公啊，
垒蛋小事你担心，
你可知，
世上还有险事情？
情势比累卵险万倍，

告诉你，
不知我主可愿听？”
晋灵公连连点头叫快说，
荀息说：
“怕你听后怒气生。”
灵公连说不生气，
荀息趁机表真情：
“大王你下令修建八层台，
三年也难建成功。
这样使妇女不能把布织，
男人无法把地耕。
全国百姓都筑台，
国库很快要变空。
邻国若见我国弱，
就会发兵来进攻，
那样晋国会灭掉，
你看这算不算险情？”
晋灵公听到这里已醒悟，
忙下令废了建台的错决定。
“危如累卵”这成语，
比喻事物处于极度危险中。

As Precarious as a Pile of Eggs

Duke Ling in the State of Jin during the Spring and

Autumn Period(770—476B. C.), grew corrupted after he inherited the throne. He lived a luxurious life, forgetting all about his country and people. In order to have a good time, he mustered all his ministers and gave a decree. He asked them to prepare plenty of timber, and to gather all the workers in the country. He wanted to put up a new building, and it should be finished in half a year. He knew that the ministers would oppose him, so he swore that he had made up his mind, if anyone dared to stop him, he would put him to death immediately.

There was a minister named Xun Xi, who was dutiful and tactful. He would like to see Duke Ling about this, which quite annoyed the latter. It was obvious he had come to say no to him. Duke Ling thought Xun Xi was asking for death, Xun Xi also understood it was a dangerous thing to do. So he declared when he saw the Duke: "I haven't come to persuade you, I just came to play a game with you."

Duke Ling was delighted to have heard that, and showed a smile on his face. Xun Xi took out nine eggs and 12 checkers in his hands, saying he could pile the checkers up, and then put all the eggs on the checkers. "Pile them up one by one, it will surely make Your Majesty happy!"

Duke Ling didn't think that he had ever seen it before, "all right, all right," he said repeatedly. Xun Xi held his breath for a while by his side, tenderly he

pinched the checkers, and stacked them one by one. When all the checkers were settled, he then began to stack the eggs, while all the on-lookers were holding their breath.

Duke Ling said "It's too dangerous!" Now Xun Xi opened his mouth and spoke softly: "Your Stately Majesty, piling up eggs is but a trifle thing to worry about. Do you know there are other important things to worry about that might be 10 thousand times more dangerous than that? I wonder if you'd like to hear that?"

Duke Ling nodded his head and said yes. Xun Xi said, "I fear you'll be angry when you hear it." Duke Ling repeatedly said he wouldn't be angry. Xun Xi then took the chance to tell him the truth, "Your Majesty ordered an 8-storey building to be built, and it must take 3 years to accomplish. In that way, all the women will not be able to spin, and all the men will not be able to plough. If all the countrymen are organized to build it, the National Bank will be emptied soon. If the neighboring countries see our weakness, they will attack us with their army, then the State of Jin will be eliminated. Isn't it the most dangerous thing to think about?"

Duke Ling now saw that he was in the wrong, and immediately ordered a stop to his wrong decision.

The idiom "As Precarious as a Pile of Eggs" indicates that something is in extreme danger.

七十二、刎颈之交

战国时赵国有个惠文王，
朝中有一对名将相：
蔺相如廉颇这俩人，
是赵国的玉柱和金梁。
连那秦国也不敢小看赵，
尽管它比起赵国大又强。
蔺相如廉颇一度有矛盾，
到后来前嫌顿释互谦让，
誓同生死共患难，
结成了刎颈之交人颂扬。
那蔺相如地位本很低，
后来有人把他推荐给赵王，
赵王派他带上国宝“和氏璧”，
到虎狼秦国走一趟。
因为秦王贪心大，
倚仗国强逼赵王，
想骗取赵国和氏璧，
允诺用城池交换是假装。
赵国若不送玉去，
又怕秦国来打仗；
送玉究竟委派谁？
蔺相如经人推荐才把重任当。

秦廷没有辱使命，
“完璧归赵”人颂扬。
有一次秦赵两王渑(miǎn)池会，
秦王想当众辱赵王，
反被相如巧奚落，
想吃甜头却把苦头尝。
蔺相如两次立大功，
赵王便封他为国相，
位居上卿地位高，
官职竟在廉颇上。
廉颇也曾为国立大功。
凭战功才把大将当。
出生入死经百战，
不服气相如为国相。
他认为相如只凭一张嘴，
真正本事无一样。
廉颇说以后遇相如，
要给他一点厉害尝。
这话儿传到相如耳，
相如根本不放心上。
有一次见廉颇骑马从前边来，
气势汹汹朝前闯，
丝毫没有相让意，
相如就先朝一边让。
别人都以为相如心胆怯，

相如说廉颇将军比秦王哪个强？
秦王他那样厉害我都不怕，
我怎会见了将军心发慌？
之所以见了将军先避开，
我是考虑到国事上。
假如是我们二人闹矛盾，
那只会有利于秦王。
蔺相如明理明义一席话，
廉颇闻听愧得慌。
他袒露上身负荆条，
请罪亲到相府上。
将相和好嫌隙去，
结成了刎颈之交情意长。
生死与共朋友情，
以此形容最恰当。

A Ready-to-Behead-for-You Friend

During the Warring States Period (475—221B. C.), the king of the State of Zhao was Huiwen. In his court he had two famous ministers: One was Lin Xiangru and the other was Lian Po. Both of them were the backbones of the state. With the two at home, even the State of Qin wouldn't look down upon the State of Zhao, though it was much stronger.

Lin and Lian were once at a discord, but later

they reconciled and united, and became sworn friends, to be praised by later generations. It was said that Lin Xiangru was at a low status, when he was recommended to the king of the State of Zhao. The king asked him to take the famous "Heshi Jade", and go on a diplomatic errand to the State of Qin.

The king of Qin was very greedy, and used his power to bully the king of Zhao. He cheated to obtain Zhao's "Heshi Jade", by pretending to offer one of his cities. The State of Zhao indeed didn't want to give the jade, but they feared that Qin would thence attack them. But who could take up this mission? Lin Xiangru was recommended to do the job. He lived up to his task in the court of Qin. "Returning the Jade Untouched" was spoken highly then after.

The next time at Mianchi there was a summit, Qin's king wanted to insult Zhao's king publicly, only to find himself teased by Lin Xiangru, obtaining trouble instead of taking advantages. So Lin Xiangru was double-awarded, and the king appointed him prime minister, prior to all the ministers, and superior to Lian Po the general.

Lian Po had also achieved a great deal for the country, only by this he was awarded the title of general. Having braved his life and fought hundreds of wars, he didn't disagree with Xiangru's being a prime minister. He thought that Lin was only using his

mouth, and there was nothing that could be called a real stuff. He said that if he met with him some day, he would give him an insult.

When Xiangru heard about this, he didn't mind at all. One day he saw Lian Po coming head-on, furiously driving along, meaning nothing at all of making way for him. So Xiangru had to move aside. People thought Xiangru was afraid of him. Xiangru then asked who was more fearful, General Lian Po or the king of Qin?

"I don't even fear the king of Qin at all, how could I be timid before the general! The reason I made way for him was just for the sake of the interest of the country. If we two were ploughed in a discord, that would be beneficial to the king of Qin." That reasonable speech of Lin Xiangru's threw Lian Po into deep sorrow. He then came to Lin's residence to proffer a birch and ask for a flogging. Minister and general were now reconciled, and became bosom friends ready to die for each other.

If you would like to denote two sworn friends, just remember to use this idiom!

七十三、瓮中捉鳖

元朝有位杂剧作家康进之，
曾编过《李逵负荆》这出戏。
演的是北宋末年天下乱，
农民们纷纷闹起义。
就在山东梁山泊，
有许多英雄好汉来聚义，
为首的大名鼎鼎叫宋江，
正筹划进一步扩大根据地。
靠水泊有一个村子叫杏花庄，
庄头上开一个酒店悬酒旗。
开店的老板叫王林，
年纪也有六十几。
有一个女儿名叫满堂娇，
父女俩相依为命过日子。
有一天两个流氓进店来，
耍无赖就把老汉女儿欺。
这俩贼自称都是水泊人，
假冒鲁智深宋江俩人名。
老王林女儿遭灾心悲痛，
正哭时李逵下山到这里。
老王林一番哭诉激英雄，
黑好汉信以为真生怒气，

似旋风回到梁山寨，
忠义堂前拿板斧劈，
一斧砍倒杏黄旗，
逼宋江去和王林亲对质。
到后来事情真相弄大白，
方知道，罪犯是流氓和地痞。
错怪了哥哥非小可，
最不该一怒砍倒聚义旗。
好李逵脱去上衣负荆条，
找宋江认错又赔礼。
宋江说，真正坏人未捉到，
光是赔礼有啥用！
恰巧是王林上山来报告，
说坏蛋又到他店里。
他女儿也被带了来，
俩坏蛋已被灌醉在梦里。
宋江叫李逵快去捉坏蛋，
李逵说，瓮中捉鳖很容易。
飞快去抓来坏蛋正了法，
李逵也深深受教育。
“瓮中捉鳖”作成语，
常比喻坏人早已被控制，
逃跑已是不可能，
若要捉住很容易。

Catch a Turtle in a Jar

In the Yuan Dynasty (1271—1368A. D.) there was a playwright by the name of Kang Jinzhi. He composed a play titled "Li Kui Apologizes". It tells the story of the warring Northern Song Dynasty. The peasants had an uprising now and again. It was by the water margin of Liangshan in Shandong Province. Many a hero gathered together. The commander is the famous hero named Song Jiang, who was planning to enlarge his base. Beside the water margin there was a village named "Almond Blossom Village". In front of the village there opened a restaurant. The proprietor of the restaurant was Wang Lin. He was already in his sixties. He begot a daughter named Man Tangjiao (meaning dear in the whole house). Father and daughter lived a well-to-do life.

One day two hooligans came into the restaurant, and shamelessly took the girl away. They called themselves Lu Zhishen and Song Jiang, two masters from the troop on the water margin. Old Wang Lin was crying over the disaster when Li Kui got there having come down from the mountain of the water margin. Old Wang's sad story stirred up the hero. This black guy assumed it true and got furious, and in quite a whirl he went back to the quarters, raising his ax in front of the "Loyalty and Humane Hall". He felled the

apricot-yellow flag, and forced Song Jiang to confront Wang Lin.

Later they knew what the truth was. The criminals were two scoundrels. It was terrible to wrong my dear brothers, and it was even more terrible to fell the flag. The smart man bare-backed proffered a birch, and asked Song Jiang for a flogging. Song Jiang said that now that they had not caught the bad guys, what was the meaning of the apology. Just then Wang Lin came to report, that the two scoundrels haunted his restaurant again. His daughter had been brought here, and the scoundrels had been made drunk to sleep. Song Jiang asked Li Kui to catch the bad guys. Li said it would be just like catching a turtle in a jar. He promptly went there and crushed the robbers to death, and drew from it quite a good lesson.

"Catch a Turtle in a Jar" as an idiom indicates the bad men have already been under control. As it is impossible to flee, you can easily take hold of them.

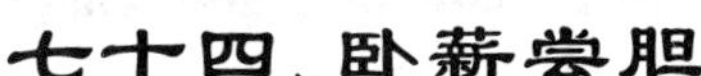

七十四、卧薪尝胆

春秋时吴越两国起征战，
越王被吴王打败输得惨。
吴国的国王叫夫差，
越国的国君名勾践。
吴王夫差曾把勾践捉回国，
简直把越王当作猪狗看。
到后来越王设谋回国后，
发愤图强报仇怨！
每天夜晚他睡在柴堆上，
头上方悬挂一只苦猪胆。
睡觉前先要尝尝苦胆味，
时刻把国耻家仇记心间。
经过数年努力后，
勾践与以往不一般，
治理得民富国也强，
伺机领兵报仇怨。
终于把吴国消灭掉，
后人提起总称赞。
把“卧薪尝胆”作成语，
比喻人刻苦奋发能自勉。

Sleep on Brushwood and Taste Gall

During the Spring and Autumn Period (770—476B. C.), there was a war between two states: Wu and Yue. The king of Yue was defeated by the king of Wu. The name of the king of Wu was Fu Chai, and the name of the king of Yue was Gou Jian. Fu Chai had once arrested Gou Jian and taken him to his country, and treated him as a dog or pig. Later the caught king managed to get back to his home country. He resolved to take revenge. Every night he slept on brushwood, and every night before sleep, he would taste the pig's gall hanging overhead, remembering the shame of his country and foe of his family.

After several years of hard work, Gou Jian turned out to be a new man. He ran the country well and his people were all rich, and he was preparing for revenge. In the end he wiped out the State of Wu. People in later generations often praised him.

"Sleep on Brushwood and Taste Gall" as an idiom indicates one should work hard and be self-reliant.

七十五、吴牛喘月

晋初的一天，满奋去见武帝司马炎，
武帝指着北窗口椅子让他坐，
北窗口立一个透明琉璃屏风扇。
看上去只有一个空框子，
窗外景历历在目随意观。
尚书令自幼体弱最怕风，
天气冷他就不敢坐窗前。
无奈是皇帝坚持要他坐，
满奋正处在进退两难间。
晋武帝忽想起满奋的怕风症，
估计是屏风的琉璃他没看见，
便手指着屏风笑起来。
满奋也知心思被看穿，
在皇帝面前尴尬闹笑话，
弄得他神情窘急心不安。
他说道："臣子我好比吴地的牛，
怕热天，见到了明月也气喘。"
到后来，"吴牛喘月"作成语，
常形容心神不定情绪乱。
这样的人由于害怕某事物，
恰巧再遇这事物迹象显，
由于他心里常处戒备中，

遇到了自然心惊战。

The Water Buffalo of Wu Region Panting at the Moon

One day in the early Jin Dynasty (265—420A. D.), secretary-in-chief Man Fen went to see Emperor Wu, Sima Yan. The emperor pointed to the chair beside the northern window and asked him to sit down. The window had a transparent glass screen, so it looked just like an empty frame, and the scenery outside was clear to see. The secretary-in-chief was feeble early from his childhood and had wind-panic. It was cold then, and he didn't quite dare to sit near the window. But the emperor, His Majesty did ask him to sit down there, and this put him quite in a dilemma.

The emperor suddenly remembered Man Fen's wind-panic disease. Thinking that he didn't see the transparent screen, he pointed at the glass and burst into laugher. The secretary-in-chief knew too that he was seen through. Fearing he would make himself a fool before His Majesty, he just didn't know how to react. He then said, "I am just like the water buffalo of Wu Region, Your Majesty, fearing the sun's heat, panting at the sight of the moon!"

Later, "the Water Buffalo Panting at the Moon" became an idiom, which can depict that someone is

feeling upset. When those who fear something see that thing appear, with their subconscious always on the trigger, they inevitably feel afraid.

七十六、五十步笑百步

世上常有这样的人，
动不动就会讥笑人。
即使是他也有错误和缺点，
也要讥笑和他同类人。
他认为自己的过失无所谓，
找错误常把双眼盯别人。
就好像古时候打仗短兵相接，
有的人打败了拖枪逃遁。
甲跑了一百步然后停下，
乙跑了五十步也自站稳。
乙往往要嘲笑甲是胆小，
讥讽甲打仗时害怕敌人。
事实上五十步百步都是逃，
不能以逃快逃慢把害怕分。
逃跑均是因害怕，
硬说五十步比百步英勇实在不准。
朋友们请分辨然后记牢，
千万不要做乙那样的人。

One Who Retreated Fifty Paces Mocks At One Who Retreated One Hundred

There are such people in the world, who tend to mock at other people occasionally. Though they themselves have their own mistakes, they just laugh at their like. They take for granted that they are flawless, and they are always finding fault with others. This is like the case when in ancient times at war, the defeated soldiers were running crestfallenly. A Mr. A had run one hundred paces and then stopped, a Mr. B had only run fifty paces and then stopped. Then Mr. B laughed at Mr. A and said that Mr. A was a coward, and that Mr. A was the most timid on battle field.

My dear friends you can judge that and keep in mind, never try to be a Mr. B.

七十七、惜墨如金

北宋初年有位画家叫李成，
在当时的画坛很有名，
尤其他的山水画。
最受画界人推崇，
他描摹北方山野寒林景，
用墨讲究淡与浓。
像风雨明晦烟云雪雾等天气，
出自他笔下有特征。
独到之处人称妙，
"惜墨如金"赞李成。
"惜墨如金"作成语，
常比喻写字绘画作诗文，
落笔着墨最谨慎。

Use Ink as If It Were Gold

In the early Northern Song Dynasty (960—1127A. D.) there was an artist named Li Cheng. He was well-known in the circle of arts. He was especially good at landscapes. He was admired for depicting the northern mountains and forests in winter. He dwelled much on the lightness and heaviness of the ink's hue, so as to describe wind and rain, bright and

dark, smoke and clouds, snow and fog etc. They were all stylistic. People praised him for his unique technique. They said that he used his ink as if it were gold.

"Use Ink as if It Were gold" as an idiom is indicating that one should be very serious, when painting or writing poetry and literature.

七十八、笑里藏刀

唐朝时有个大臣叫李义府，
最谙熟奉承拍马术。
唐高宗非常喜欢他，
官封中书还不满足。
平时他见人面带三分笑，
表面看温和谦恭有礼数，
内心里十分阴险和毒辣，
坏主意经常往外出。
有一次一个妇女犯了法，
被关进了监牢待惩处。
李义府听说此女很漂亮，
就设法把狱卒收买住，
甜言蜜语哄又诓，
让狱官把那妇女罪名除。
这个妇女刚放出，
便有人把她送李府。
李义府这个色鬼占了她，
她才知免罪有缘故。
过不久有人告狱吏私下放犯人，
李义府假装不知还生嗔怒。
那狱吏心想早晚会受牵连，
更了解心狠手辣反复无常的李义府，

吓得偷偷上了吊，
李义府却装作啥事无。
有个叫王义方的气愤不平，
便把全部情况揭发出。
李义府知道此事后，
心气恨表面却看不出，
背地里去见唐高宗，
说王义方十恶不赦净坏处。
唐高宗生气罢了王义方的官，
发配到边远地方去受苦。
时间久人们知道这件事，
都咒骂笑里藏刀的李义府。
"笑里藏刀"这成语，
常喻人外表和善心歹毒。

Hide a Dagger Behind a Smile

In the Tang Dynasty (618—907A. D.), there was a minister named Li Yifu, who was skilled in flattery. The emperor Gao Zong liked him very much, and appointed him as a secretary, but he was not contented. He always carried a smile on his face, and looked as if he was gentle, prudent and polite. He was actually very mean in the heart, and wicked ideas constantly came out of his head.

Once a woman broke the law, and was jailed

waiting to be punished. Li Yifu overheard that this woman was very beautiful. So he managed to buy over the prison guard. He lulled and coaxed him with sweet words, making him remove the woman's accusation. As soon as she was released, the woman was brought to Li's residence. Not until the erotic Li Yifu took advantage of her, did the woman know the reason for being free. Before long the prison guard was accused of illegally releasing criminals. Li Yifu pretended to know nothing about it and showed his anger about it. The prison guard had thought it would happen sooner or later, and deeply knew about Li's wickedness, so he had to hang himself secretly. As for Li Yifu it seemed nothing had happened.

There was a man named Wang Yifang who was indignant about it, and he laid bare all and all. When he got to know that, Li Yifu was furious inside but showed nothing outside. When he had a private audience with the emperor Gao Zong, he bad-mouthed Wang Yifang and said he was downright evil.

This threw the emperor into a fury and removed Wang Yifang's post, and sent him into exile in a far away place. By and by people came to know about that, and they cursed Li Yifu saying he hid a dagger behind a smile.

"Hiding a dagger behind a smile" as an idiom, denotes someone is kind outside but wicked inside.

七十九、欣欣向荣

陶渊明是东晋末年的大诗人，
他写的田园诗篇很出名。
晋安帝文熙元年十一月，
陶渊明正在彭泽县衙中。
做官已经有三月，
经常气得肚子疼。
他看不惯官场那一套，
上司来他耻于去接迎。
他不愿同流合污混在浊世，
时刻想辞掉这小县令。
这一天天气十分好，
他坐上了小船便启程。
把那颗象征生杀予夺权的铜官印，
端端地放在书房中。
没啥行李与财物，
来时空空去也空。
船儿顺风跑得快，
不觉半天到家中。
归家后写了一首诗，
《归去来辞》是诗名。
诗中写热爱人民和自然，
流露着思念田园的真感情。

诗中写有人告诉他，
开春的田野正春耕。
他也欣然同前往，
看不够欣欣向荣春日景。
万象更新花草茂，
万木欣欣正向荣。
到后来"欣欣向荣"作成语，
常用它把草木的生机来形容。
也可以用来作比喻，
喻事业昌盛和繁荣。

All Is Thriving

Tao Yuanming was a very famous poet in the late Eastern Jin Dynasty (317—420A. D.). He was well-known for his idylls. In the 11th month of the first year of Emperor Jin An, Wenxi, when Tao Yuanming was head of Pengze County, he had been in his post for just three months, and it frequently made him sick in the stomach. He didn't appreciate the way other officials performed, and he felt ashamed to receive his superiors. He couldn't float with the indecent tide of the society, thinking all the time to quit the post.

One day the weather was very fine, and he made his voyage on a little boat. The copper official seal, which bore authoritative power, was lying peacefully

in his study and he didn't take much of his luggage, lightly he came and lightly he went. The boat moved very fast before the wind, and he reached home in half a day before he realized it.

He wrote a poem after he got home, and "Returning Home" was its title. In the poem he depicted his love for the people and the nature, showing nostalgia and the pastoral emotions. In the poem he said that he was told, that the farmers were ploughing the present spring season. He went ecstatically with them to the fields, enjoying the thriving scenery of the spring flowers and grass engendered with 10 thousand living things, 10 thousand trees are merrily shooting.

Later "All is thriving" became an idiom, it means the grass or the trees are energetically growing. It can also be figuratively used, to denote something is prosperous.

八十、行尸走肉

东晋时有名学者叫王嘉，
传世之作叫《拾遗记》。
书中讲有个书生叫任末，
非常用功肯学习。
可惜没固定的老师可请教，
只好四处去拜师。
小任末当时只有十四岁，
肩挑着行李和书籍，
不怕路途多险阻，
小小年纪有志气。
他常说："人生如果不学习，
干事业怎会有成绩！"
后来任末长成人，
教书谋生挣衣食。
他一边教导学生把书读，
自己还坚持苦学习。
他选取风景优美处，
搭起一间小茅屋，
平时生活多艰难，
连纸笔灯油也买不起，
他便借月光星光来读书，
拿荆木削尖当作笔。

他读书还有个好习惯，
读到那精彩句段便停止，
顺手抄在衣襟上，
以便温习能牢记。
学生们被他的精神所感动，
就经常为老师做新衣。
任末晚年临终时，
给学生留下谆谆告诫深道理：
好学者虽死犹未死，
不学者虽生犹死尸。
到后来“行尸走肉”这成语，
常把庸碌无能之辈比，
以及那精神贫乏无寄托，
或反动愚蠢之辈也可比。

A Walking Corpse

In the Eastern Jin Dynasty (317—420A. D.) there was a scholar named Wang Jia, who wrote a masterpiece entitled “Anecdotes”. In his book he told that there was a student named Ren Mo, who studied very hard. It was a pity that he hadn't got a constant teacher, so he had to travel about to find one. At that time he was only 14 years old. He carried his luggage and books with a shouldering-pole. He didn't fear the long hard journey, for he had high goals. He would

say that if one didn't study, how could he manage to succeed in his work.

Later when Ren Mo grew up, he earned a living by teaching. He worked hard to teach himself, while he taught his students. He chose a beautiful place, where he set up an awning. He was constantly hard up in his life, he could not afford pens and paper and lamp oil, so he had to read and write in the moonlight, and he sharpened a wattle from a tree to use as a pen.

He had a good habit in reading. When he came across interesting sentences or paragraphs, he would jot them down on the lining of his coat, so as to review them afterwards. The students were so moved by his spirit, that they frequently tailored new clothes for their teacher. Before Ren Mo died in his advanced age, he gave his students his sworn words. A well-educated man died an immortal death; Whereas an ill-educated man was like a walking corpse.

Later on "A Walking Corpse" became an idiom, referring to those good-for-nothing ones, and also it can be used to scold some reactionary pinheads.

八十一、胸有成竹

宋朝时有位画家叫文同，
他的画就数画竹最成功。
为什么他画竹子那样好？
据说他能把竹子印心中。
平日里仔细观察多用心，
画出来犹如真竹一般同。
到后来“胸有成竹”作成语，
常常把这样的情况来形容：
做事情事先考虑很周密，
到时候才有把握得成功。

Having an Image of Bamboo in the Mind

In the Song Dynasty (960—1276A. D.) there was an artist named Wen Tong. He was famous for his skills of drawing bamboo. Why could he draw them well? It was said that he had already printed the images in his mind. In his daily life he observed them very carefully, so he could draw them lifelike.

Later on, "Having an Image of Bamboo in the Mind" became an idiom, and it is often used in this way: One should have a well-thought-out plan beforehand in order to turn it into reality.

八十二、揠(yà)苗助长

古时候有个农夫很愚蠢，
做事情轻重缓急不能分。
有一天他到田里看庄稼，
见禾苗长得太慢心恼恨。
他心想不如挨株拔一拔，
一用劲苗儿果然高几分！
这个人整整拔了一上午，
累得他浑身是汗腰腿酸。
回家后对着妻儿瞎吹嘘，
夸自己拔苗助长大本领。
他儿子不信此话下田去，
见禾苗全被太阳晒蔫巴。
这说明做事切忌凭主观，
违背了客观规律受惩罚。
“揠苗助长”作成语，
“揠”的意思就是拔，
拔苗助长不现实，
客观规律永远要遵循。

Try to Help the Shoots Grow by Pulling Them Up

In ancient times there was a very foolish farmer. He was muddle-headed about what he was doing. One day he went to the fields to see his crops, only to find them grow very slowly and he was annoyed. He thought to himself, I should pull them up one by one. Oh, the shoots did grow higher with his efforts. This guy pulled and pulled for the whole morning, and he was all knocked out. He bragged to his wife and children when he got home, that how smart of him to make all the shoots in the field grow much faster. His son, however, didn't believe him and went to the fields, and saw all the shoots were withered in the sun.

This indicates that one shouldn't be too subjective, and he should be punished if he goes against the natural law.

八十三、言过其实

公元 228 年的一天，
诸葛亮带兵打祁山，
那时候三国鼎立势已成，
祁山属于魏国管。
诸葛亮身为西蜀相，
有一位将领他很喜欢，
这个人名字叫马谡(sù)，
自恃才高很健谈。
自以为兵书读得不算少，
经常对用兵打仗陈己见。
尽管是孔明对他很器重，
刘玄德却深知马谡有缺点。
刘备在临终前反复叮嘱诸葛亮，
说马谡之才很一般，
言过其实不虚心，
使用一定要慎重点，
切不可委以重任去领兵，
诸葛亮却并不以为然。
过不久任命马谡做参军，
经常跟他把兵书谈。
这一次孔明带兵打祁山，
先锋官，大家都估计是魏延。

没想到孔明竟然封马谡，
叫他领兵走在前，
还让他立了军令状，
可马谡，全不把魏兵放心间。
到后来丢失街亭要塞地，
被魏兵杀败实在惨。
诸葛亮又一次伐魏成泡影，
退回汉中把气叹。
军纪军法当严肃，
只得忍痛含泪把马谡斩。
“言过其实”作成语，
常形容不切实际尚空谈。
言语夸大吹牛皮，
必然失败落笑谈。

His Words Are More than His Real Talent

One day in the year of 228 A. D. , Zhuge Liang led his troops to attack Qishan Mountain. At that time, the Three Kingdoms had already formed the pattern of tri-pot. Qishan was the territory of the kingdom of Wei. Zhuge Liang, the prime minister of the kingdom of Shu had one favourite general by the name of Ma Su, who was quite self-confident and had a silver-tongue. He was so well-read about the art of war that he often stated his strategies before battles.

Although Zhuge Liang liked him very much, Liu Bei knew very well Ma Su had shortcomings. Before his death Liu Bei repeatedly told Zhuge Liang that Ma Su was only a common talent. His words were more than his real talent and he knew nothing about modesty. He told Zhuge Liang to be careful of him, and he should not trust him as much as to appoint him to too high a post. But Zhuge Liang didn't take it seriously. Before long he appointed Ma Su as a military consultant, and talked often with him about the art of war.

At this time Zhuge Liang led the troops to attack Qishan. The pioneering general was generally thought to be Wei Yan, but surprisingly, Zhuge Liang named Ma Su, and let him march in the front. He had even signed a guarantee. But Ma Su turned a blind eye to Wei soldier's powerfulness. In the end the important fortifier Jieting was lost, and his soldiers were seriously beaten. Zhuge Liang's plan to attack Wei turned to soap bubbles, and he sighed his sorrow after retreating to Hanzhong. The military laws and regulations should be taken seriously, so he had to behead Mu Su with tears in his eyes.

"His Words Are More than His Real Talent" became an idiom denoting those who are talkative but not pragmatic, who brag and boast and blow very hard, only to meet their failure and remain a laughing stock.

八十四、掩耳盗铃

从前有个人，想偷大铜铃，
只因铜铃大，力小背不动。
正在急迫时，陡然巧计生：
何不用铁锤，砸碎那铜铃？
砸成小块块，运走准轻松。
铁锤才一击，铜铃发响声。
响声震人心，耳朵嗡嗡嗡。
忽又心生计，何不把耳蒙，
蒙耳听不到，别人不惊动，
大胆把铃砸，不由喜心中。
铜铃已砸碎，不闻铃响声，
终被人捉住，公堂受酷刑。
到后来"掩耳盗铃"作成语，
常讽刺糊涂人自作聪明把自己哄。

Plug the Ears While Stealing a Bell

Once there was a man who wanted to steal a bell. The bell was too big and he was too weak to move it. He was worrying when an idea occurred to him. "Why not use a hammer to break the bell? Break it into pieces and it could be easy to carry." Just as he struck, the brass bell rang, which was heart-stricken and ear-split-

ting. Then flashed another idea: "Why not plug my ears? With my ears plugged, others wouldn't be wakened." Boldly he broke the bell and he was ecstatic. The job was smartly done and no one had heard. But he was caught red-handed and seriously punished.

Then "Plug the Ears While Stealing a Bell" became an idiom, deriding those foolish men who intend self-deceit.

八十五、叶公好龙

古时候有个叶公喜欢龙，
他家里处处都能见到龙：
不光是家具件件刻上龙，
就连那房梁屋柱也刻上龙。
这件事被天上的真龙知道了，
就想看看这位叶公。
有一天龙驾祥云来找叶公，
降落叶公庭院中。
龙头从窗口伸进屋，
龙尾巴就在院中直摇动。
叶公他见了魂魄早吓跑，
钻床底下浑身乱抖动。
到后来“叶公好龙”作成语，
常把那虚假的爱好来嘲讽。
如果有人表面喜好某事物，
便可用这条成语来形容。
“叶公”式人物经常能遇到，
朋友们千万不要学叶公。

Lord Ye's Love for Dragons

In ancient times there was a lord Ye who loved

dragons. You could see dragons everywhere in his home—not only on every piece of his furniture dragons was carved, but on every ridge and every post of the house, too. When this was known by the real dragon in heaven, he flew over to his courtyard on a cloud, and wagged his tail in the middle of the yard. When Lord Ye saw this he was petrified, and crawled under the bed and shook all over.

Later "Lord Ye's Love for Dragons" became an idiom, ridiculing those who have some professed love. If someone loves something only in the appearance, you can use it to describe him.

八十六、一鸣惊人

春秋时，楚庄王即位三年整，
整日处在沉默中。
政事从来不料理，
也不给臣下发命令。
右司马看在眼里急在心，
想劝庄王勤理政。
有一天，他要给庄王讲故事，
语调自如又轻松，
庄王微微把头点，
表示愿意静心听。
司马讲南山有种鸟，
已落山上三年整，
既不展翅学高飞，
也不登枝唱歌声。
讲完后笑问庄王为什么？
庄王回答带笑容：
“此鸟三年未展翅，
只因羽翼未长成；
此鸟三年不鸣叫，
是体察事理观民情；
此鸟不飞并非笨，
一飞必冲九霄云；

此鸟不鸣并非哑，
一鸣定使众吃惊！
你的意思我明白，
请卿静候观动静。”
这话说过半年后，
庄王亲自来理政，
他废止了十项旧制度，
建立了九项新章程，
诛杀了五名不法臣，
任用六位贤德隐士做大臣。
从此楚国得大治，
庄王之举果英明。
“一鸣惊人”作成语，
常比喻经过充分准备后，
才会有惊人的大成功。

Give the World a Shock with a Single Singing

During the Spring and Autumn Period (770—476B. C.), King Zhuang of Chu had been on the throne for three long years, but he only remained silent in the court. He didn't handle state affairs, and never gave orders to his subordinates. The prime minister was worrying in his heart, and tried to persuade him to pay more attention.

One day he was telling King Zhuang a tale in a light and easy tune. King Zhuang was nodding gently, showing that he was willing to listen. The minister said that in the southern mountains there was a kind of bird, which had perched there for three whole years, but he remained there without stretching his wings to practice flying, nor mounting a branch to practice singing. Having finished the story, the minister asked King Zhuang with a smile what bird it was. King Zhuang answered smilingly, for three years the bird hasn't extend his wings, was only because his wings hadn't grown to full length; For three years the bird hasn't sung a note, was only because he had to make a careful study. This bird is not dumb at all, when he flies, he will soar into heaven; This bird is not mute at all, when he sings, he will give the world a shock.

"I know what you meant to say, but please just wait and see." This said, and half a year passed by, the king came to deal with the state affairs on his own. He removed ten old policies, and built up nine new ones. He put to death five unlawful ministers. He put to use six virtuous hermits. Since then the State of Chu was run quite well, and King Zhuang was a wise governor after all.

"Give the World a Shock with a Single Singing" then became an idiom, implying that he who has been

well-prepared, and can make a great achievement.

八十七、一叶障目

古时候，楚国有个穷书生，
性懒惰，不愿做工与种田，
成日里，梦想发个意外财，
发了财，好置办房屋与田产。
这一天，他翻阅古书《淮南子》，
见书上，讲到螳螂会捕蝉，
螳螂捕蝉能隐形，
树叶遮体蝉不见。
这书生，读到这儿心一动，
跑出书房树底站。
事情说来也真巧，
书生果然有发现：
院内那株古槐上，
有只螳螂正捕蝉！
螳螂隐在树叶后，
蝉正鸣唱未看见。
螳螂叶后伸大钳，
一下钳住那只蝉！
书生两眼瞅得准，
爬到树上摘叶片。
不想心慌手发抖，
叶片飘飞落地面。

许多落叶混一起，
那片神叶难分辨。
无奈何，把树叶统统扫进屋，
一片一片手中掂，
掂起树叶问妻子：
“我在这里你可见？”
妻子回答“能看到”，
书生又把树叶换。
妻子觉得很奇怪，
问丈夫，为何老把树叶玩？
书生光笑不回答，
又把树叶举面前，
又问妻子能见否？
五遍十遍不嫌烦。
妻子见此心生气，
索性回答“看不见”。
书生一听真高兴，
忙把那叶藏袖间。
第二天，他喜滋滋地出了门。
奔到集市人堆钻，
手里高举那片叶，
以为人家看不见，
伸手去拿摊上货，
卖货人，一把抓住高声喊：
“大家快来抓小偷！”

人群围得铁桶般。
这个书生被抓住，
送进县衙公堂站。
这故事，让你笑后生思索，
想一想，书生为何落笑谈？
只因为，一叶障目迷心窍，
千人万眼丑态现。
树叶一片遮视线，
眼前泰山全不见。
常比喻，局部现象把人迷，
整体大局难顾全。
认识处理问题时，
往往盲目和片面。

A Leaf Before the Eye Hinders the Sight

In ancient times, there was a poor scholar in the State of Chu. He was too lazy to work and farm, and he was always daydreaming to have a windfall someday. He hoped to get money for estate and house. One day when he was browsing the book "Huai Nan Zi", he read the message about the mantis preying on the cicada. The mantis was invisible when preying, because he had a magical leaf. This scholar was so deeply impressed that he rushed to a scholar-tree outside his study. It happened to be quite a coincidence,

but the scholar then did find in the old scholar-tree in his yard a mantis was preying on a cicada. The mantis was just behind a leaf while the cicada was singing and couldn't see it. The mantis reached his paws from behind the leaf, and caught the cicada with one stroke.

The scholar was staring at the very leaf, and quickly climbed up the tree for the leaf. Unfortunately he was too excited to hold it firm, and the leaf dropped flying onto the ground. It mixed with others on the ground, and it was very hard to tell which one was the magic one. Obligedly he had to collect all the leaves and take them inside. He picked up the leaves one by one. A leaf in hand, he asked his wife: "I'm here but can you see me?" His wife replied, "yes, I can." The scholar had to change it for another leaf. The wife found it very queer, and asked him why he was playing with leaves. The scholar however, gave her no answer but only smiles, and just put a leaf in front of him, and asked her if she could see him at all. Five times, ten times passed and he was not at all bored, but keeping-on made the wife a little annoyed. And she then bluntly gave him the answer "No, I can't see you".

The scholar was very pleased and jumped up, and immediately hid the leaf in his sleeve. The next day, he went out as happy as a lark. He went to a

county fair and joined the crowds. He held high the magic leaf, and thinking that others could not see him, he reached to steal the stock of a stall. The peddler caught him and yelled: "Someone come quick and seize the thief!" People nearby came and circled around. The scholar was caught red-handed, and taken to the court of the county.

This story makes you laugh and provides you with food for thought. Give it a thought, why the scholar was a laughing stock? It was just because the leaf before the eye, put him in disgrace before the public. A leaf before you may block your sight, and Mount Tai ahead you can't see! It means that some superficies are very confusing, and one can't easily get an overall idea. In dealing with a problem, people tend to take a one-sided approach.

八十八、一夜十起

东汉初年有个人，
复姓“第五”名叫“伦”，
为人正直性廉洁，
美名流传到如今。
曾在会(kuài)稽做太守，
家务事从不劳他人。
喂马谷草自己铡，
妻子烧饭守灶门。
朋友个个夸他说：
“第五真真无私心。”
他笑道：“莫过奖，
结论先请别忙下，
略举两例请评论：
有朋友，请我替他谋差事，
送我一匹黄骠马，
让我为他‘开后门’。
这匹骏马我没接受，
啥差事，我也没有把他任。
可是我经常还会想起他，
怕他怨我无情分。
再比如，我的侄儿生了病，
我看过回房便安寝；

可后来，我的儿子生了病，
我一夜十起看视勤。
即使这样还担心，
睡下了，也牵肠挂肚不安稳。
只这两件平常事，
你说说，我到底有无自私心？”
朋友听后很感动，
逢人便夸第五伦，
夸他真诚又直率，
实事求是看自身。
到后来，“一夜十起”作成语，
常形容，医生真诚待病人。

To Rise Ten Times in One Night

In the early Eastern Han Dynasty(25—220A. D.) there was a man whose family name was Diwu, given name Lun. He was honest and upright, and his fame comes down to the present. When he was appointed governor of Kuaiji District in Zhejiang Province, he never asked others to do his house chores. He cut grass for his cow himself, and when his wife cooked, he attended the fire for her. His friends all spoke highly of him: “Brother Diwu was really selfless.” But he smiled and said, “Don’t over-praise me. Conclusions should not be made too soon. Here I will

give two examples for you to judge. One of my friends, who wanted me to do him a favour, offered me a yellow steed, begging me to open a 'back door' for him. I refused his offer of the horse, and I didn't give him the access to any official posts. But sometimes I often think of him, and I am afraid that he might hate me. Another thing is that when my nephew was once ill, I went to see him and returned home to sleep soundly. But later when my son got ill, I rose ten times at night to tend him. And even so I was still worried about him, feeling quite upset before I fell asleep. From these two small matters in my everyday life, could you draw the conclusion that I am selfless?"

On hearing this his friends were very impressed, and praised Diwu Lun even more often. They praised him for his honesty and uprightness, and his true analysis about himself. But later "to Rise Ten Times in One Night" became an idiom, indicating a doctor or a nurse tenderly look after his patients.

八十九、咏絮之才

东晋时有一位丞相叫谢安，
谢丞相对于诗歌最喜欢。
有一天北风呼呼大雪飘，
他带领侄儿侄女赏雪玩。
俗话说“瑞雪兆丰年”，
赏雪人个个心中喜悦添。
谢安想何不对雪把诗赋，
顺便把孩子们的学问考一遍。
老丞相指着大雪笑颜开，
要孩子们一人一句作诗玩。
大侄儿谢朗知道考他们，
心里头害怕落后忙争先。
他念道：“撒盐空中差可拟”，
老谢安笑笑说道“不恰当。
瑞雪怎好比作盐？”
回头问侄女谢道韫：
“好孩子，你若想好何不念？”
道韫说：“我想的恐怕也不好，
说出来，敬请叔叔指教俺。
我说是：‘未若柳絮因风起’。”
一句诗，乐坏叔叔老谢安。
谢朗说：“妹妹诗句果然好，

柳絮比雪不一般，
风吹柳絮如飞雪。
形象生动多好看。”
丞相见侄儿评论也不差，
乐得捋须举杯盏。
如果是女孩年幼有诗才，
便与道韫是一般。

A Talent for Singing of Willow Catkins

In the Western Jin Dynasty (265—316A. D.) there was a prime minister named Xie An, who took the greatest interest in poetry. One day a strong north wind was blowing a big snow. He took his nieces and nephews to watch the snow. The old saying went that a big snow implied a bumper harvest. The snow-viewers were all very pleased. Xie An then thought to himself, "Why not let each of them make a poem about the snow? So that I can test their knowledge."

The old prime minister pointed to the snow and smiled, and asked each of them to present a poem of the snow. The eldest nephew Xie Lang knew that his uncle wanted to give them a test, but he feared that he might lag behind. He read out, "It is snowing just like distributing salt from the sky." Old Xie An laughed and said, "it isn't proper, how can you compare snow with salt?"

Turning his head back to his niece Xie Daoyun, "my good niece, why don't read out yours?" Daoyun said, "mine is not a good one either I'm afraid, and I sincerely beg your criticism." She then read from her mind, "just like catkin flying with the wind." This line made her uncle very pleased.

Xie Lang said, "my sister's line was really wonderful, comparing snow to willow catkin was quite extraordinary. It was life-like and vivid and sounded nice, too." The old prime minister noted that his nephew's review was also quite to the point. He happily stroked his beard and raised his wine cup. If you get a girl who has a poetry talent, just say that she is just like Daoyun, who has the talent for singing of the willow catkin.

九十、优孟衣冠

春秋的时候有一天，
楚国有个小孩在路上玩，
突然间草丛窜出一条蛇，
跑到他前头把路拦。
平常之蛇孩子不害怕，
可这一条生得不一般：
蛇身长着两个头，
四只眼睛朝孩子看。
这孩子猛记起一句迷信话，
说谁见了双头蛇会把阎王见。
他心想若这话儿是真的，
今天我可怎么办？
自己死了倒无所谓，
怕就怕以后还有人看见。
谁要见了就遭殃，
遗患无穷心不安！
这少年拾起几块石块儿，
豁出性命和蛇战。
终把那蛇打死后，
挖坑深埋在里边。
回家后把这件事告诉老母亲，
母亲听罢直称赞。

后来这少年并未死，
还一天天地长才干。
家庭教育本就好，
他个人努力也不一般。
到后来楚庄王任他做相国，
才能学问得施展。
他帮助楚王料理国家事，
声名在楚国到处传。
他便是楚相孙叔敖，
《史记》里头有他的传(zhuàn)。
谁料到孙叔敖自从逝世后，
楚庄王慢慢把他的功劳全忘完。
连他的妻儿也不过问，
孙家人生活很艰难。
孙叔敖的儿子只好上山去砍柴，
挑上大街换油盐。
这件事被一个名叫孟的人听到，
这人在宫廷做演员。
古时候演员被人称为“优”，
人家就把他“优孟”喊。
优孟是个热心人，
生就的侠肠和义胆。
孙叔敖还在世上时，
曾给儿子留遗言：
以后如果有困难，

进宫去找优孟谈。
这一天孙叔敖的儿子果然来，
优孟立刻把他见，
答应了保证替他想办法，
让他回家等着看。
优孟便回想相国孙叔敖，
面貌神情在脑中现。
他模仿叔敖的神态和动作，
一年里几乎天天练。
直练得举止全像孙叔敖，
这才把孙相当年的服装换。
恰遇着王宫开宴会，
优孟便去把楚王见。
俯身把壶满酒时，
楚王抬头猛看见。
楚王不由吃一惊，
以为孙叔敖复生在眼前，
便求他再来做相国。
优孟故意头不点，
求楚王允他先回家，
跟妻子商量商量看。
三天后优孟复来见楚王，
说妻子对此有意见。
妻认为楚相做不得，
楚王一听更纳罕。

优孟说：
“比如说已故相国孙叔敖，
他生前功劳重如山。
大王你得以霸诸侯，
他死后，
你竟把他忘一边。
连他的遗属也不问，
他的儿子赡养老母亲，
打柴糊口真可怜。”
楚王听了优孟的话，
再仔细朝这人脸上看，
发现他根本不是孙叔敖，
原是优孟巧装扮。
紧接着优孟又细对楚王讲，
说孙叔敖家境如何难。
楚王大大受感动，
很快给孙叔敖儿子封了官。
到后来“优孟衣冠”作成语，
常形容某人能乔装会打扮；
也比喻文艺作品缺乏创造性，
一味模仿无主见。

Actor Meng in Costume

One day during the Spring and Autumn Period

(770—476B. C.), a boy was playing on the road in the State of Chu, when suddenly emerged from the grass a snake, running ahead and getting in his way. Snakes he generally never feared, but this one was particular. It had two heads on its body, and gazed at him with its four eyes. The boy then remembered the superstitious saying: "He who encounters a snake with a double head will soon go to hell." And he was wondering if it was true. "What shall I do? It's no pity if I alone am dead, but what if others see it? For whoever sees it, they must die. For this I really feel upset."

This lad then picked up some little stones, and fought furiously with the snake. In the end he beat it to death, and dug a hole and buried it there. He told his mother about it when he got home, and his mother was very pleased with him. Later on this boy didn't die, but grew smarter and smarter day by day. He certainly received an excellent education at home, and he made extraordinary efforts in his studies, too. Later King Zhuang made him premier, so that he could make full use of his talent. He helped King Zhuang run the state very well, and his fame spread to the four corners of the State of Chu. He was known as Premier Sun Shu'ao, and "The Records of the Historian" recorded his biography. But unfortunately after he passed away, King Zhuang gradually

forgot all of Sun's achievements, and gave no thought of his widow and children, and so they all had a hard life.

Sun Shu'ao's son had to go collecting wood in the mountains, and then traded it in the streets for food, oil and salt. This matter was heeded by a man named Meng, who served as an actor in the palace. At that time actors were called "*you*". So people called him You Meng (Actor Meng). You Meng was a man of golden heart, born with a particular mind. When Sun Shu'ao was still alive, he made a will to his son. If he should come across any difficulty, go and tell You Meng about it.

One day Sun Shu'ao's son did come to see him, and You Meng received him immediately, promising him that he would do something for him, and asked Sun's son to go home and wait. You Meng recalled the late premier Sun Shu'ao, his voices and smiles reappeared in his mind. He imitated Sun's manners. On each and every day of the year, until he looked in every way just like a Sun Shu'ao, did he change into the uniform that Sun once wore.

It was just on one of the court-party days that You Meng went to see the King of Chu. He was bending to pour wine for the king, when suddenly the king caughtsight of him and got a surprise. Thinking that Sun Shu'ao had come back to life again, he asked

him to be the premier again. And You Meng deliberately gave a positive answer, saying that he had to go home first, and consult with his wife before he made such a decision.

Three days later, You Meng came back to meet King of Chu again, and he said that his wife was opposed to this idea. Hearing that the wife would not allow her husband to be the primier, the emperor was even more puzzled. You Meng then explained, "take Premier Sun Shu'ao for example, he had gained mountainous achievements, but when Your Majesty obtained sovereignty over all the dukes, you forgot all about him, and Your Majesty, you forgot his widow and children too. They had to make out a living by collecting wood." When the King of Chu heard this, he made a careful study of Meng's face, and found he was not Sun Shu'ao at all, he was only You Meng in disguise.

Then You Meng gave the king more details, telling him that Sun's family was in great difficulty. The King of Chu was deeply moved, and assigned Shu'ao's son an official post immediately.

Later on "the Actor Meng in Costume" became an idiom, referring to someone in disguise. And it can also be used to denote creativity deficiency of some literary and artistic works, which imitate others all along.

九十一、愚公移山

古时候有太行王屋两座山，
两山都在冀州南。
有一位北山愚公九十多，
面山居住出门难。
这天他唤来儿孙召开家庭会，
号召大家齐挖山。
儿孙们或者反对或赞成，
他老伴心里装个大疑团。
第二天他带领儿孙动了手，
挖的挖来担的担。
要把这大山全部搬到海里去，
出门走路才方便。
有一个寡妇的孩子来帮忙，
被叫做智叟的老头先看见。
智叟说愚公家白费气力瞎逞能，
老老小小根本不能把大山搬。
愚公一听不服气，
歇下担子和智叟辩。
愚公说："你这老头不晓事，
瞎说胡道目光短浅。
你须知，俺死了还有俺儿子，
儿孙后代传万年。

这山虽大难再高，
搬掉一点少一点！”
愚公他不理智叟松劲话，
带领儿孙干得欢。
这精神感动天上玉帝后，
派来了两位好神仙，
把两座大山全搬走，
愚公门前现青天。
这说明做事必须有毅力，
不怕困难和艰险。
坎坷过后有坦途，
勇气毅力是关键。

The Foolish Old Man Removed the Mountains

In ancient times there were two mountains: Wangwu and Taihang, both located in the south of Jizhou. An old man in his nineties who lived to the north of the two mountains, confronting them, imposing on his family much inconvenience.

One day, he called his sons and grandsons together and held a family meeting. He called on them to remove the mountains. Some of the members were for and some were against it, and his wife was the most doubting. The following day he led his children

and grandchildren to work, to dig the stones up and to carry them away. They were determined to carry the mountains to the sea, so that it would be convenient for them to go out and come in.

A small boy with a widowed mother came to their help, while an old man named "Wise Old Man" took notice of all this. The "Wise Old Man" stated that they were all trying in vain, with all his young and old members. The Foolish Old Man was not easy to get over. He rested his shoulder-pole and argued with him. The Foolish Old Man said, "You old muddle-head, you only know that under your nose, you must remember that if I die my son lives. My sons and grandsons will go on for ever. Though this mountain is very high, it can be removed little by little."

The Foolish Old Man totally neglected the Wise Old Man's discouraging words, and kept on digging perseverantly. The Foolish Old Man's spirit moved the Jade Emperor in heaven so much that he sent two angels down there, and carried the two mountains away, showing blue skies to the old man's doorway.

This story indicates that we need quite a dose of willpower in our work, fearing not difficulties and hardships. Passing through the rough road and then to the smooth and even trip, courage and perseverance are the key points.

九十二、鱼目混珠

有一部古书叫《玉清经》，
里头有一个故事很动听，
讲的是有位古人叫满愿，
有一次买了颗大珠心高兴。
珠大直径有一寸，
平时收藏密室中。
一般人轻易见不到，
越这样显得越贵重。
他有位邻居叫寿量，
有一颗特大的鱼眼睛，
他以为也是颗大珍珠，
也把它藏在密室中。
有人要来看一看，
他连连摆手说不行，
还说满愿的珍珠我也有，
从今后不能由他独逞能。
说起来事情真够巧，
不久后他俩得了同一种病。
医生给他们诊断后，
配药时要珍珠粉末当药引用。
他们俩把收藏的珍珠齐拿出，
寿量的珠假不能用。

"鱼目混珠"这成语，
常比喻以假乱真、以次充好把人哄。

Pass Away Fish Eyes as Pearls

There was an ancient book entitled "The Book of the Clear Jade", and in it there was a very terrific story. It tells that there was a man named Man Yuan. One day he merrily bought a very big pearl. This pearl had a diameter of one inch, and was carefully stored in his secret cellar. That common people couldn't see it, made the pearl even dearer.

Man Yuan's next door neighbor named Shou Liang, who has a huge fish eye, he assumed that it was a big pearl, too. He also put it in his cellar secretly. If anyone came to try to take a look, he would repeatedly shake his head. And he said that what Man Yuan had he had too. From that day on he could share the glory of owning a rare treasure.

It happened just one of these days, they contracted the same ailment at the same time. The doctor diagnosed them and prescribed for them, they both should have pearl powder as the medicinal usher, so they both took out their treasures at once, but Shou Liang's pearl just didn't work. "Pass Away the Fish Eyes as Pearls" became an idiom, which means to pass off something sham as genuine.

九十三、鹬(yù)蚌相争，渔人得利

从前有条小河旁，
河蚌沙滩晒太阳，
天上飞只凶鹬鸟，
见到河蚌喜得慌，
落下忙把蚌肉啄，
蚌嘴猛合鹬叫嚷：
“你把俺嘴夹住了，
赶快松开疼得慌！”
河蚌紧夹不放松：
“到你死时俺才放！”
鹬鸟性急也发怒：
“三日不雨有死蚌！”
正当双方在争执，
那边过来打鱼郎。
渔夫见状心欢喜，
急走上前捉了双。
这个故事有意义，
朋友切切记心上，
渔人唾手能得利，
只因鹬蚌不相让。

When the Snipe and the Clam Grapple, It's the Fisherman Who Stands to Benefit

Once upon a time beside a little river, a clam was lying on the sand in the sun. In the sky a snipe was flying over, and he was very pleased when he saw the clam. He abruptly dove down to peck the clam's flesh, and the clam promptly closed his shell and the snipe yelled: "you have clamped my mouth, let it go quickly, it hurts."

The clam fastened his shells, "I'll not let it go until you are dead!" The snipe was now also very furious. "For three days if there is no rain, there will be a dead clam!" Just as they were holding on, along came a fisherman from a distance. The fisherman was very glad, and he rushed forward to catch both the snipe and the clam.

This story is interesting and meaningful. You must keep it in mind my friend, why the fisherman found it easy to obtain the benefit—It was just because the snipe and clam didn't compromise.

九十四、欲加之罪，何患无辞

故事发生在公元前651年的秋天，
晋国的献公刚死去，
国家无主人心乱。
献公的儿子好几个，
到底由谁来"接班"？
宫廷内部有争斗，
一时半会尚未完。
有个公子叫奚齐，
献公疼爱心眼偏。
昏庸的献公临终时，
曾叫人把大夫荀息唤，
把自己的打算说给荀息听，
要荀息辅佐奚齐好好干。
还有个大夫叫里克，
对这种做法有意见。
他想让公子重耳继王位，
对荀息这人他看不惯。
晋献公死后奚齐即位没几天，
里克便杀死了奚齐要造反。
荀息又立了公子卓，
里克又杀死了新王手不软。
荀大夫孤掌难鸣也自杀，

晋国一时闹大乱。
过不久公子夷吾又即了位，
可在位的时间也很短。
到后来公子重耳回了国，
决心彻底绝内患。
他要把里克先处死，
里克当然有意见。
重耳说："你废除过奚齐和公子卓，
不杀你恐怕我将来也有那一天！"
里克说："如果我不那样做，
主公你怎么会有现在这一天。
看起来你想要治我的罪。
没有理由也照样办！"
里克自知难免死，
只得自杀赴黄泉。
到后来里克的话变成语，
比喻那些害人的人，
想害人就随意干。
"欲加之罪，何患无辞"，
就是定罪名时不容他人来分辩。

If You Are Out to Condemn Someone, You Can Always Trump up a Charge

This story took place in the autumn of 651 B. C.

when Duke Xian of the State of Jin died. The country went into chaos for losing its ruler. Duke Xian had several sons, but who was the qualified heir that would inherit the throne? There was a conflict in the court, which couldn't be ended very quickly. One of the princes was named Xi Qi, and he was Duke Xian's favourite. When the muddle-headed Duke was dying, he had minister Xun Xi called for. He told Xun Xi his intention, and asked Xun Xi to carefully assist Xi Qi. Another minister named Li Ke, was oppossed to the decision. He would like Prince Zhong Er to take the throne, and Xun Xi minded this man quite a lot. Only a few days after Duke Xian's demise and Xi Qi's taking the throne, Li Ke killed Xi Qi and held an uprising. Xun Xi then helped Prince Zhuo to the throne. Li Ke then killed the new duke without mercy. Minister Xun was put back in the corner and committed suicide, and then the State of Jin plunged into chaos. Before long Prince Yi Wu mounted the throne, but he only remained on it for a very short time. Then Prince Zhong Er came back from outside the state, and resolved to put the State in order. He intended to put Li Ke to death, which made Li Ke very sad. Zhong Er said "you have deprived Princes Xi Qi and Zhuo, and I am afraid that someday you'll deprive me, too."

Li Ke said, "if I hadn't done that, how would it have come to you now. So it seems to me that if you

are out to punish me, you can just do it for no reason at all." Li Ke knew that he must die, and he committed suicide at last.

Later on, what Li Ke had said became an idiom, denoting those who want to do harm to others, could do as they please. To condemn someone, you can always trump up a charge. Trump up a charge allowing no explanations.

九十五、余音绕梁

古时候，
有一位歌手叫韩娥，
想到齐国去谋生活。
半途中干粮吃完盘缠尽，
就到那乡村集镇去唱歌。
唱歌时向人讨点钱与物，
人都说，
从未听过这么好的歌：
歌喉优美多动听，
齐国无人比得过。
传说韩娥离去后，
那歌声余音三天不停歇，
回响在屋宇梁柱间，
给人欢愉和快乐。
“余音绕梁”作成语，
常比喻，
优美歌声音袅袅，
给人印象很深刻，
艺术享受最难得。

The Music Lingering Around the Beams

In ancient times, there was a singer named Han E, who wanted to make a living in the State of Qi. On the way she ran out of food and money. She had to go to villages and towns to give performances. She sang songs and got some money or supplies, and people said that they had never heard such fine singing. Her voice was amazingly beautiful. No-one in the State of Qi could compare with her. It is said that after Han E had gone, for three days the music had been lingering around the beams of the house, supplying people with joy and pleasure.

"The Music Lingering Around the Beams" became an idiom, indicating some beautiful music keeps carrying on, giving a deep impression to its audience, as a great artistic pleasure.

九十六、运斤成风

从前楚国的郢(yǐng)都有个好工匠，
工匠姓石会使斧，
使斧头的技艺实在神奇。
有个人想试试他的真本领，
就把工匠请回家，
在鼻子上抹了一块白灰泥，
灰泥在鼻尖像苍蝇翅，
叫工匠用斧头给他砍下去。
这工匠抡起斧头一阵风，
砍掉灰丝毫没有伤到鼻尖皮。
巧工匠砍罢提斧头站一旁，
那个人佩服得了不得。
古代"斤"字本指斧，
"运斤成风"作成语，
含义是：
本领真正学到家，
使用起来就能出神入化显神奇。
青年朋友要记住，
为了建设富强国，
我们一定要练就那：
"运斤成风"过硬的真功底。

Whirl the Hatchet Like Wind Blowing

Once in Ying City, in the State of Chu there was a good craftsman. He had a feat for using his hatchet. One day a man wanted to test his skill, and invited him home. The man put a speck of chalk on the tip of his nose, then asked the craftsman to scrape it off. The craftsman whirled his hatchet like a puff of wind, and removed every bit of the chalk without any injury to the nose. The craftsman stood holding his hatchet. The man who wanted to test him worshiped him as a real hero.

This denotes that if you practice and practice and reach perfection, miracles will surely occur.

九十七、朝三暮四

在《庄子》这部古书中，
有一个寓言故事趣味浓：
说是古代有个人，
最大的兴趣是养猴子。
别的饲料也没有，
喂猴全部用橡实。
每只猴每天早上喂三个，
晚上那顿喂四只。
过不久，猴子个个提意见，
怨恨主人太小气。
要求食物再增加，
不然抗议要绝食。
这人一听哈哈笑，
连说这是好建议。
于是他改成早上喂四个，
晚上那顿给三只。
愚蠢的猴子都高兴，
尽管肚子还会饥。
"朝三暮四"作成语，
常形容，玩弄手法把人欺，
也比喻有人经常会变卦，
做事缺乏准主意。

Three in the Morning and Four in the Evening

In the ancient book "Zhuang Zi", there was a very interesting fable. It told that in the ancient times, there was a man whose hobby was to raise monkeys. He fed them with only oak cones, and nothing else. He gave each monkey three in the morning, and he gave each four for the evening meal. By and by, the monkeys began to complain. They badmouthed their host as a miser, and they wanted more of their food, otherwise they would go on a hunger strike.

This man replied with ready laughter, and said that it was a good suggestion. Then he gave them four cones for their morning meal, and three cones for the evening meal. The foolish monkeys were all very pleased, though they were still very hungry.

"Three in the Morning and Four in the Evening" as an idiom indicates someone who blows hot and cold, or someone who chops and changes, and rides over the fence.

九十八、指鹿为马

秦朝时有个大臣叫赵高，
一心想篡夺君位把皇帝当。
可他怕众多的大臣心不服，
想试探众人对他怎么样。
有一天他让人捉来一只鹿，
赵高他亲手牵鹿进朝堂，
来到皇帝跟前指鹿说：
“臣要献一匹宝马给皇上！”
皇帝一听很生气，
责备他指鹿为马欺君王。
那赵高让周围的大臣来评说，
问他们到底是鹿还是马？
大臣们都知赵高有野心，
胆小的就随声附和说马真壮！
那正直的就说明明是只鹿，
怎能金銮宝殿哄君王？
还有人生性懒开口，
索性站立一边不声张。
到后来赵高心狠手更辣，
把那些正直的大臣全杀光！
“指鹿为马”作成语，
常比喻，颠倒是非、混淆黑白把人诳。

Call a Stag a Horse

In the Qin Dynasty(221—206B. C.), there was a Prime Minister named Zhao Gao, who was intending to usurp the power to be emperor. He was afraid that he wouldn't have the popularity with all the ministers, so he wanted to test it.

One day he had a stag caught, and drove it into the court himself. He came to the emperor and pointed to the stag and said, "I would like to present to Your Majesty a good horse." The emperor was very angry when he heard it, and condemned him for cheating the emperor by calling a stag a horse. Then Zhao Gao asked the ministers around to judge whether it was a stag or a horse.

The ministers all knew that Zhao was ambitious. The timid ones began to echo that the horse was very strong. The honest and upright ones said that it was obviously a stag, how could he take a horse before His Majesty? Some hesitated by nature, and they just remained there standing quietly. Later on Zhao Gao became even more vicious, and killed all the honest and upright ministers.

"Call a Stag a Horse" as an idiom, means something black was called white, something wrong was called right as to deceive people.

九十九、走马观花

从前有个人相媳妇，
腿脚不好是个瘸子，
担心被人家看出来，
那样人家肯定不愿意。
小伙子冥(míng)思苦想一整夜，
终于想出个好主意，
就在与姑娘相会时，
专门借匹好马骑。
远望着那边过来一娉婷(pīngtíng)，
面庞长得很秀丽。
手拿一朵玫瑰花，
放在面前闻香气。
小伙子见到姑娘这样美，
对自己双腿也不留意，
别提心中多高兴，
乐得轻声哼小曲。
那姑娘眼见一骑翩翩来，
马上端坐个小伙子，
模样英俊又威武，
不由心中生欢喜。
双方定聘下彩后，
日月穿梭过得急。

转眼已是一年整，
小伙要把媳妇娶。
择了佳期娶新人，
洞房里头闹腾腾，
众人簇拥新人拜天地，
到晚间众人散去洞房静，
小伙子把媳妇盖头忙揭起，
原来这姑娘脸盘虽然长得好，
嘴唇上边却没鼻子。
两只窟窿朝着天，
螃蟹样嘶啦嘶啦直吹气。
姑娘也朝小伙看，
两条腿一长一短是瘸子。
到后来，故事变作一成语，
“走马观花”多有趣！
既形容心情愉快人得意，
也比喻观察事物不仔细。
还说的是：
你用走马掩脚残，
她用闻花隐鼻缺，
己短可以掩，
他残也难见。
巧掩短来巧亦拙，
男女双方都傻极！

Ride a Horse to Look at Flowers

In ancient times, a man went to find his would-be-wife. He was lame in one leg. He feared that he might be found out, and that they wouldn't permit the marriage. He thought and thought for a whole night, and he thought out a very good idea. On that very day, he borrowed a good horse to ride. He saw from a distance a fair lady with a very very beautiful face. She was holding a rose in her hand, and was smelling it.

Our young lad found his young beauty. Forgetting all about his lame leg, he felt like he was in heaven, and he started humming melodious music. This lass was noticing this gentle rider sitting graciously on horseback. He was strong and handsome, and she was overjoyed in the heart. Then they engaged with each and other, and time went by like a moving shuttle. Very soon one year had passed. Our lad wanted to make our lass his bride. The wedding day saw a crowded wingding. People huddled there to give them a wedding ceremony.

By night, they left the couple in their room. The lad hurriedly pulled off the bridal face-cover, and found out that although the bride's cheeks were good-looking, she hadn't got a nose. The two nostrils were opening skyward, and they blew out air just like a

crab's mouth. The lass was looking at this lad, and found him lame with one leg long and one short.

Later, this story turned into an idiom. What fun is it to see someone riding a horse to look at flowers. That may mean someone is very glad, or someone gains a shallow understanding from a fleeting glance. It also implies that: You can hide your lame leg by riding on horseback; She can cover her broken nose by smelling the flower. Your shortcomings can be hidden; Other's flaws can be invisible, too. The skill you use to hide the flaws is a flaw indeed.

一百、坐山观虎斗

春秋时期有一天，
在鲁国境内有一座山，
山上两只凶恶的大老虎，
老虎把一头老牛腿咬断。
咬死了老牛撕牛皮，
顷刻之间肉吃完。
吃完肉两只老虎咬起来，
一大一小猛开战。
小的哪是大的敌，
喉咙管一口被咬断。
尽管小虎被咬死，
大虎也受伤直喘气，
这时候那边冲来一猛士，
挥剑直把虎喉穿。
大虎受伤难招架，
被猛士刺死在山边。
猛士名叫卞庄子，
已经观斗整一天。
“坐山观虎斗”作成语。
常形容甲乙双方争斗时，
丙不介入只旁观。
待它两败俱伤时，

丙再从中捡便宜。

Sit on Top of the Mountain to Watch the Tigers Fighting

One day during the Spring and Autumn Period (770—476B. C.), on a mountain in the State of Lu, two furious tigers broke the legs of an ox, killed it and devoured it. They ate up all the flesh soon, and then the two tigers began biting each other. The two biting tigers, one was big and the other was small.

How could the small one deal with the big, and its throat was soon torn off. Though the small tiger was at last killed, the big tiger was gasping exhaustedly. Just then a hunter came up over, and held out his sword to stab the tiger's throat. The tiger was too tired to resist, and was killed by the hunter at the foot of the mountain. The man's name was Bian Zhuangzi. He had been watching the tigers fighting for a whole day.

Later "Sit on Top of the Mountain to Watch the Tigers Fighting" became an idiom, and passed from mouth to mouth. It denotes when two parties are in a fight, a third one doesn't get in but only looks on, and when he sees both of them are on the decline, he takes advantage of them in the end.